Form L 31

# Hertfordshire County Library
## COUNTY HALL HERTFORD

This book should be returned on or before the
latest date entered below

Please renew/return this item by the last date shown.

So that your telephone call is charged at local rate,
please call the numbers as set out below:

| From Area codes 01923 or 0208: | From the rest of Herts: |
|---|---|
| Renewals: 01923 471373 | 01438 737373 |
| Enquiries: 01923 471333 | 01438 737333 ✗ |
| Minicom: 01923 471599 | 01438 737599 |

L32b

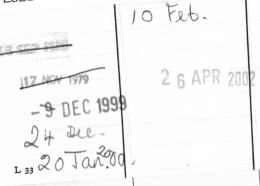

10 Feb.

13 SEP 1991

17 NOV 1979

2 6 APR 2002

-9 DEC 1999

24 Dec.

L 33 20 Jan 2000

# THE CORONATION SERVICE OF
# HER MAJESTY QUEEN ELIZABETH II

THE PROCESSION FROM THE TOWER TO THE PALACE OF WESTMINSTER

# THE CORONATION SERVICE OF HER MAJESTY QUEEN ELIZABETH II

WITH
A SHORT HISTORICAL INTRODUCTION
EXPLANATORY NOTES
AND
AN APPENDIX

BY

EDWARD C. RATCLIFF

*Ely Professor of Divinity in the
University of Cambridge*

LONDON
SOCIETY FOR PROMOTING CHRISTIAN KNOWLEDGE

CAMBRIDGE
AT THE UNIVERSITY PRESS

1953

PUBLISHED BY
THE SOCIETY FOR PROMOTING CHRISTIAN KNOWLEDGE
AND THE SYNDICS OF THE CAMBRIDGE UNIVERSITY PRESS

U.S.A.: Cambridge University Press, 32 East 57th Street, New York, 22

Canada: The Macmillan Company

Printed in Great Britain at the University Press, Cambridge
(Brooke Crutchley, University Printer)

# CONTENTS

## INTRODUCTION

*page* 35

## THE FORM AND ORDER OF THE SERVICE
THAT IS TO BE PERFORMED AND THE CEREMONIES THAT ARE
TO BE OBSERVED IN THE CORONATION OF
HER MAJESTY QUEEN ELIZABETH II

*page* 67

### APPENDIX

## THE CEREMONIAL DIRECTIONS
## OF 'LIBER REGALIS'
TRANSLATED INTO ENGLISH

# ILLUSTRATIONS

Both illustrations are taken from Egerton MS. 3320, in the Library of the British
Museum, which appears to be an incomplete draft of a Book of Ceremonies
prepared for the Coronation of Queen Elizabeth I.

# PREFACE

THIS SMALL BOOK makes no pretence at being a work of research. It offers no new discovery. Its purpose is to assist the unlearned towards a general appreciation of the Coronation Service of Queen Elizabeth II in its relation to its predecessors, and also towards an understanding of the religious ideas, under the influence of which the Coronation tradition was conceived and fashioned, and which continue to inspire the latest revision of the rite. For the Coronation is no mere ceremonial parade. It is a Service of the English Church and State. To consider it otherwise is to miss or mistake its meaning.

The author expresses his grateful acknowledgements to the Director and Principal Librarian of the British Museum for permission to reproduce the two illustrations in this book; also to the Oxford University Press for permission to quote from Dr P. E. Schramm's *History of the English Coronation*; to Messrs Constable and Company for their generous permission to draw freely on Mr Wickham Legg's *English Coronation Records*; and to Messrs Macmillan and Company for permission to cite a passage from Greville's *Journal*.

Finally, he records a debt of gratitude to the Cambridge University Press for the despatch with which they have printed this volume; and to Mr D. M. Freegard for patient assistance in proof reading.

# INTRODUCTION

THE PRACTICE of inaugurating a new Sovereign, or Head of a people, with some special observance has been universal from the earliest times. The character of the observance has varied according to the traditions of the people concerned; it may be a complex of ceremonies extended over a series of days, or it may be a simple ceremonial act capable of being performed within the space of a few minutes. It has varied also with the nature of the Headship assumed, according as the Head is considered to be military or religious, or a combination of the two, or to be solely civil or secular. The obvious appropriateness of the practice is attested by its persistence to our own time. Not all Heads of modern States are crowned; but none enters upon office without formality. Queen Elizabeth II of England is unique among the Rulers of the world in that she is anointed and crowned with solemn rites and ceremonies which represent more than a thousand years of the history and traditions of her people.

## I. THE INAUGURATION OF BRITISH KINGS

We know nothing of the method used for inducting pre-Christian British Kings in this island. We know but little more of the practice in regard to Christian British Kings. Our presumption that the inauguration would have a religious aspect, however, is borne out by a passage in Adamnan's *Life of St Columba*.[1] Adamnan records that there appeared to Columba the vision of an angel who held in his hand 'a glass book of the Ordination of Kings'.[2] The book contained a direction to Columba to 'ordain' Aidan as King. Columba had been unwilling to do this; but he submitted to the direction, and having come to Iona, he met

[1] For the Latin text, see *Adamnani Vita S. Columbae*, ed. J. T. Fowler, 1894; for an English version, see *The Life of Saint Columba, written by Adamnan*, by W. Reeves, 1874.
[2] Bk. III, ch. v.

Aidan, and 'laying his hand upon his head, he ordained him and blessed him'. Aidan was made King of Dalriada, the modern county of Argyll, in 574.

It has sometimes been assumed that 'a book of the Ordination of Kings' was a service-book containing an early equivalent of our modern 'Coronation Service'. The assumption is hasty. The Latin words for 'ordination' and 'ordain' (*ordinatio, ordinare*) are neutral, meaning simply 'appointment to office'; they do not necessarily imply that the ceremony of Aidan's appointment was an ecclesiastical rite, or service, comparable with the 'ordination' of a clergyman. On the other hand, the ceremony was undoubtedly religious and Christian. Further, there is no hint that the ceremony was unprecedented or unusual, or other than to be expected.

It has sometimes been assumed, again, that a practice of appointing new Kings by anointing them with oil prevailed in southern Britain, if not beyond the Cheviots. The argument is based upon a passage of the British monk Gildas, an older contemporary of St Columba, who, from his place of refuge in Armorica, or Brittany, wrote a highly coloured denunciation of the iniquities of southern British rulers. These Kings, he says, 'were anointed Kings not by God, but to stand out as more unmerciful than the rest, and a short while afterwards they were butchered by their anointers, not for putting truth to test, but because others more ruthless had been chosen'.[1] The phrase 'were anointed Kings' (*ungebantur reges*) is reminiscent of the biblical narratives recording the anointing of David, Solomon and others to kingship over the Hebrews. Yet no safe deduction as to southern British practice can be drawn from Gildas's phraseology. His style is rhetorical, and abounds in biblical expressions and metaphors. Also, there is no evidence that anointing with oil as a method of king-making was anywhere else in use in the early or middle sixth century. It is probable that Gildas's phrase was no more than a biblical expression borrowed to indicate appointment to office. It is admittedly difficult, however, to resist the inference that Gildas's words contain an allusion to the employment of some

[1] Gildas, *De excidio et conquestu Britanniae*, 106, ed. Th. Mommsen, *Monumenta Germaniae Historica*. Auctorum Antiquissimorum, XIII, 82.

religious ceremony at the inauguration of the Kings whom he denounces.

When Gildas wrote, the Christian traditions and institutions of southern Britain were soon to disappear, or to be preserved in isolation among the hills and mountains of Wales. The Saxon invasions had begun. Saxon settlements were being established; and the foundations of Anglo-Saxon kingdoms were being laid. It is from the Anglo-Saxons that the English Coronation tradition derives its origin.

## II. EARLY ANGLO-SAXON INAUGURATION: THE INTRODUCTION OF THE ANOINTING WITH OIL

Of the ceremonies attending the accession of a pre-Christian Anglo-Saxon King we have only indirect intimation. When the dying Beowulf, in the heroic poem of that name, recognizes the young Wiglaf as his successor, he delivers to Wiglaf his own golden neck-ring, his own gilded helmet, ring and corslet, bidding him use them well.[1] This delivery of accoutrements appears to be the outward and visible sign of the transmission of the chieftain-ship. It is probable that it conformed with common usage; and that new Kings, when they assumed their function, were invested, or invested themselves, with armour. From *Beowulf* also we learn of the throne in which the King sat when he banqueted with his warriors in the royal hall.[2]

The first recorded instance of a Christian Anglo-Saxon King being elevated with a religious ceremony belongs to the year 787. In that year, according to the *Anglo-Saxon Chronicle*, Offa, King of the Mercians, designated his son Ecgfrith as his successor, and Ecgfrith was anointed with oil. There is every reason to believe that this was an innovation in the practice of Anglo-Saxon royal inauguration, and that it was borrowed from Frankish usage, into which it had been introduced some thirty-five years previously, in order to secure the kingship of Pippin. Pippin possessed no claim to rulership by virtue of royal descent; though the actual exercise of power was his, as Mayor of the Palace he was nominally

[1] *Beowulf*, xxxviii. For a translation, see that by R. K. Gordon in *Anglo-Saxon Poetry*, Everyman's Library, 1950.
[2] iii.

the subject of the Merovingian King, Childeric III. Such an arrangement was patently unsatisfactory. With the consent of Pope Zacharias, Childeric was accordingly set aside: and at Soissons in 751 Pippin was first elected and inthroned King of the Franks in Childeric's stead, and then was anointed with oil by the Papal delegate, the Englishman St Boniface, Archbishop of Mainz, assisted by Frankish bishops.

The new ceremony is plainly imitated from the biblical usage already mentioned. Yet it seems to have been a particular rather than a general imitation. We shall probably be right, if we take the account of Solomon's anointing as David's successor, recorded in I Kings i as supplying the immediate inspiration of the events at Soissons. There is a certain parallel between the cases of Solomon and Pippin on one side, and between the cases of Adonijah and Childeric on the other. Solomon's right to the kingship, like Pippin's, was open to challenge. Adonijah, like Childeric, not only had the better natural right to be considered King, but was recognized actually to have been elevated to the kingship. At the instance of Nathan the prophet, however, assisted by Zadok the priest, David was induced to reverse his sons' roles and to prefer the younger over the elder. Adonijah, though acknowledged as King, had not been anointed. Zadok the priest, therefore, assisted by Nathan the prophet, anointed Solomon without delay. The ceremony was decisive in Solomon's favour. The people acclaimed him with the cry, 'God save the King', as they had acclaimed Adonijah not long before. Adonijah himself accepted Solomon's elevation: 'thou knowest that the kingdom was mine, and all Israel had set me over them to be their king: but the kingdom is transferred and has become my brother's: for it was appointed to him by the Lord'.[1] In these words Adonijah avows that anointing with oil confers an inviolable title to, or possession of, the kingship, his own right and previous elevation notwithstanding. As Solomon in virtue of the ceremony was 'Christus Domini', 'the Anointed of the Lord' and undoubted King, so also was Pippin. It is worthy of attention that the narrative of Solomon's elevation has given two anthems to the Coronation Service: 'Zadok the priest and Nathan the prophet anointed Solomon King', etc., sung after the

[1] I Kings ii. 15. The English rendering is here made from the Latin Vulgate.

4

Anointing, and 'Be strong and of a good courage', etc., sung after the Putting on of the Crown. Both these anthems came into the English Coronation in the tenth century from a Frankish source which probably contained elements already traditional in the Frankish rite.

Pippin was anointed a second time in 754, on this occasion by the Pope himself, Stephen II, and in the church of the old Merovingian royal foundation, St Denis; his two sons, Charles, afterwards known as 'the Great', and Carloman were anointed with him as his successors. In 771, when Pippin and Carloman were dead, Charles was sole undoubted King of the Franks. Ten years later, in 781, Charles in his turn had his two sons, Pippin and Louis, anointed to be his successors by Pope Hadrian I at Rome. In submitting his son, Ecgfrith, to the anointing, the Anglo-Saxon Offa was doubtless moved by a desire to model his domestic procedure upon that of the renowned Frankish king. At the same time, he wished to preserve the Mercian succession within his own family: and the family history of the early Carlovingians must have suggested to him that benefits of a practical kind were the consequences of anointing.

Although, however, the anointing may have appeared to Offa, and to the other Anglo-Saxon Kings who received it, to be something of an insurance for the stability of a ruling family and its kingdom, it could only appear to be so because of its sacred character. The ceremony of the anointing was a specifically religious ceremony, performed by the bishops; in consequence, it contained religious implications of importance for the kingship. The Church was not slow in drawing attention to this aspect of the matter. The ecclesiastical Synod of Chelsea, held in 787, and to which Offa himself subscribed, before proceeding, in Canon 12, to stress the honour and dignity of the 'Christi Domini',[1] 'the Anointed of the Lord', as it terms the Kings, is at pains to express, in the preceding Canon, the kind of moral and religious conduct required of them. They are to 'conduct their government with great prudence and in obedience to the divine law (*disciplina*) and

[1] For Canons 11 and 12 of the Council from which this and the succeeding quotations are derived, see Haddan and Stubbs, *Councils and Ecclesiastical Documents*, vol. III, p. 452f.

to judge with justice'. They are also to 'obey their bishops from the heart and with great humility, because to the bishops are given the keys of Heaven, and they have the power of binding and loosing, as it is written, "Ask thy father, and he will declare to thee; thy elders, and they shall tell thee".... And it has been said by the prophet, "The lips of the priest (*sacerdotis*)[1] shall keep knowledge, and they shall seek law at his mouth, because he is the messenger of the Lord of Hosts".'[2] The Council therefore exhorts the Kings to 'honour the Church of God, which is the spouse of Christ, not to lay an unjust yoke of servitude upon it, not to pride themselves in worldly power, not to oppress others by force; but rather to deserve that it should be said of them by God, "I have found a man after my heart, who performs all my will; therefore I will lay help upon him that is strong, and them that hate him I will put to flight, that he may portion out long life and the happiness of the kingdom to himself and to his children's children"'.[3] Finally, the Council enjoins the Kings to take to themselves 'wise counsellors who fear the Lord and are men of honourable life, to the end that the people, being instructed and made strong by the good examples of Kings and chiefs, may prosper to the praise and glory of Almighty God'. The 'Anointed of the Lord', therefore, had a divine duty, as well as a divine right. Inevitably, the biblical practice of anointing brought with it the biblical conception of the Ideal King, who stood in special relation to God as His Servant, and whose duty it was to defend true religion, to support its ministers, and to maintain justice and righteousness among his people. 'In few countries, if any,' to quote Mr R. H. Hodgkin, 'has the co-operation between State and Church been more harmonious, more prolonged and on the whole more fruitful than in England during the four and a half centuries between the coming of Augustine and the Norman Conquest.'[4] The adoption of anointing strengthened that co-operation, and made it yet more fruitful. The anointed Anglo-Saxon King was more than the supreme chief of his people, their military leader and their upholder against their enemies. He was

[1] The word *sacerdos* can be used to designate a bishop as well as a priest.
[2] Deuteronomy xxxii. 7, Malachi ii. 7.
[3] Cf. Acts xiii. 22, Psalm lxxxviii. 22, 24.
[4] *The History of the Anglo-Saxons*, 1935, vol. II, pp. 455 f.

King 'by the grace of God',[1] and the 'Protector of God's Church and People'. In the several 'estates of men' in the Church, he held an estate peculiar to himself, that of 'Christian King'.

The modern English forms of the Anglo-Saxon words used to indicate the King's anointing are 'hallowing' and 'blessing'. These two words, in their turn, represent the Latin *consecratio*, 'consecration', and *benedictio*, 'benediction'. Both these words are employed in the Pontificals, or Bishops' Service-books, of the tenth and later centuries as titles of the rite in which the King is anointed and crowned. They are employed, also, of those Services in which bishops and priests are ordained and consecrated, and in which they too are anointed with oil. Some writers have attempted to perceive in this fact evidence that the Anglo-Saxons intended a parallel between the act of king-making and ecclesiastical ordination, and in particular that they regarded the King's anointing in the light of the bishop's consecration. The evidence of the earlier liturgical MSS. however, lends scant support to this view. It is true, indeed, that the practice of anointing both priests and bishops had made its appearance in the second half of the eighth century; yet the practice was not universal in the West until a later period. Priests were the first recipients of anointing. The anointing of bishops was borrowed from the ordination of priests. Both orders originally received anointing on their *hands*. Kings, on the other hand, received anointing on their *heads*, in accordance with the Hebrew usage described in the biblical narratives. By *circa* 800, there is evidence that some Frankish bishops were anointed on the head; but the practice was not approved by Charles the Great, who regulated the liturgical procedure of his dominions by the usage of Rome. Roman usage at that time knew nothing of ordination anointing.[2] The evidence of the Service-books of this period suggests that, as the anointing of the bishop's hands was copied from that of priests, so the anointing of his head was copied from that of Kings.[3] The history of these ceremonies was soon

[1] This phrase, still included in the Sovereign's title, was in use in England earlier than elsewhere.

[2] The practice of anointing has never been adopted by the Greek Orthodox Church either for the ordination of clergy or for the inauguration of emperors.

[3] For a discussion of this subject, see G. Ellard, *Ordination Anointings in the Western Church before 1000 A.D.*, Mediaeval Academy of America, 1933.

7

forgotten. Some three centuries afterwards, when, by concurrent processes of elaboration, the two Services of the King's coronation and the bishop's consecration had acquired a distinct resemblance to each other, it is no matter for surprise that the ceremonies of coronation should be supposed to have been modelled upon those of the bishop's consecration, and that a congruous theory of the King's quasi-ecclesiastical status should be formulated by those who had a political interest in doing so. To attribute the liturgical resemblances and the theory founded upon them to the Anglo-Saxons of the eighth and ninth centuries, however, would be anachronistic. To the Anglo-Saxons of that time, the King's 'hallowing' was *sui generis*; it was a 'consecration' indeed, but a consecration to Christian Kingship.

### III. THE FIRST ENGLISH CORONATION SERVICE, A.D. 973

Of any prayer or other ceremony which may have accompanied the anointing of Anglo-Saxon Kings in the eighth and ninth centuries, we have no evidence. It is possible, and not improbable, that the act of anointing was associated with the putting on of the royal helmet and investiture with other armour. The crown seems not yet to have come into use. It is true that Queen Judith, the second wife of King Ethelwulf, was both anointed and crowned at her marriage at Verberie in 856. The rite followed for this ceremony was Frankish, like Judith herself. The anointing of Kings' consorts was not at this time in accordance with Anglo-Saxon usage; and the occasion of 856 was too much of an innovation for us to conclude that it represents the adaptation of practice normally followed at the inauguration of a King to the case of a queen-consort.

The first English Coronation Service, properly to be so called, was drawn up for the coronation of King Edgar in Bath Abbey on Whitsunday, 973. Edgar succeeded his brother Eadwig in 959, and was the first King of All England. For some reason he was not anointed at his accession. The eleven years' interval gave St Dunstan, whom Edgar had made Archbishop of Canterbury, opportunity to think carefully about the rite of Edgar's anointing, whenever it should take place. During his exile at Ghent, Dunstan had

8

become acquainted with continental precedents. Several possibilities were before him. Two early coronation rites, apparently for Anglo-Saxon use, are still in existence. Dr P. E. Schramm supposes them to be drafts prepared by Dunstan before reaching a final decision.[1] The first, which has affinities with Queen Judith's rite and is preserved in the Exeter Service-book, known as the *Leofric Missal*,[2] limits the ceremony to anointing, after the early Anglo-Saxon tradition. The second, preserved in the so-called *Pontifical of Egbert*,[3] adds to the anointing the delivery of Sceptre and Rod and the putting on of the royal helmet. It also inserts the rite into the Mass, so that it follows the Gospel, an arrangement which is parallel with that of the Service for consecrating bishops. Possibly both St Dunstan and King Edgar regarded the anointing as a sort of ordination: 'it is probably something more than a mere coincidence', to quote Sir F. M. Stenton, 'that the year of [Edgar's] coronation was the year in which he reached the age of thirty, below which no one could canonically be ordained to the priesthood'.[4] In the final form of the rite, however, this arrangement was abandoned, partly, perhaps, because it implied more than was intended or desired. The anointing and investiture of 973 were placed before the beginning of the Mass, a position which they were to retain up to 1661.

The Coronation of 973 began with a procession in which Edgar was conducted to the church by nobles, clergy and nuns, to the singing of an anthem. Two bishops on either side of the King led him by the hand. When he entered the church, he removed his 'diadem', and prostrated himself before the altar, while *Te Deum* was chanted. *Te Deum* ended, he was formally elected by the bishops and the people. Thereupon, he made his Promise, which is the earliest form of the Coronation Oath (see below, p. 24). Several prayers followed, the last of which was the solemn 'Consecration of the King', closing with a petition that he might be anointed 'with the oil of the grace of the Holy Spirit'. The King

[1] *A History of the English Coronation*, 1937, p. 19.
[2] See F. E. Warren, *The Leofric Missal*, 1883, pp. 230ff.
[3] Ed. by W. Greenwell, Surtees Society, vol. 27, 1853; the text and a translation of the 'Egbert' recension are printed in L. G. Wickham Legg, *English Coronation Records*, 1901, pp. 3–13.
[4] *Anglo-Saxon England*, 1950, p. 363.

was then immediately anointed on the head, to the singing of the anthem, 'Zadok the priest and Nathan the prophet', etc. Next, he was invested successively with the Ring, the Sword (which was girt upon him to the singing of the anthem 'Be strong and of a good courage', etc.), the Crown, the Sceptre and the Rod. Each act of delivery was accompanied by an address and a prayer expressing the religious and moral symbolism of the object delivered. The ceremonies ended with a lengthy benediction of the King and with the charge, 'Stand firm and hold fast from henceforth the state', etc., presumably pronounced as the King sat in his throne.[1]

The Mass, with Proper Collects and Preface, was then sung; and a banquet followed the Mass.

The meaning of the Service of 973 is clear. It did not make Edgar King; he had been King for eleven years. The 'election' was his formal acceptance by Church and people. In the Promise he had bound himself to his people to govern christianly. The anointing gave him what he had not received before: consecration to government. The delivery of Ring, Sword, Crown, etc., was investiture with the outward signs of royalty. The effect of the rite as a whole was to confer upon the King a new status: he was now confirmed in his dignity by divine sanction, and was made the mediator between the clergy and the laity, of whom also he was to be the defender. In a word, he had become a Christian King.

In drawing up this Service, Dunstan borrowed freely from continental coronation rites. The Ring, the Sword, the Sceptre and the Rod were all derived from Frankish usage. The Crown itself was the emperor's diadem, which could claim the further sanction of biblical precedent. The prayers and addresses were variously derived. Yet Dunstan's work is far from being a mere mosaic. Dr P. E. Schramm has described it as 'a very rich ceremonial which could stand comparison with the Frankish and German'; and he continues, 'the balance and happy arrangement of the *ordo* of "Edgar" made it superior even to the models upon which it was based'.[2] St Dunstan's Service gave to the English Coronation Tradition, at its very beginning, a broad pattern, which it has preserved for almost a thousand years.

[1] For the text and a translation, see L. G. Wickham Legg, *English Coronation Records*, pp. 15–29.    [2] *A History of the English Coronation*, pp. 20f.

## IV. MEDIAEVAL REVISION AND ELABORATION: THE CORONATION SERVICE OF *LIBER REGALIS*

The 'Edgar' Service of 973 was used for the Coronation of William the Conqueror on Christmas Day, 1066, William claimed to be the lawfully appointed successor of King Edward the Confessor; and it was therefore appropriate that he should be crowned by Edward's tomb in Westminster Abbey, which was Edward's church. His two successors were also crowned at Westminster. In this way were laid the foundations of the right of Westminster Abbey to be the coronation church of the Kings of England. A century later, the Abbot and Convent of Westminster were recognized as being the proper guardians of the royal ornaments, or *Regalia*, so that the Crown, the Rod, and other objects used in the rite came to be described as 'St Edward's'. The status thus acquired by Westminster Abbey was the means of settling a disputed matter. Westminster is within the Province of Canterbury. In consequence, the office of consecrating and crowning the King devolves exclusively upon the Metropolitan of that Province, the Archbishop of Canterbury, or, in the event of his incapacity to act, upon another of its bishops.

In the course of the twelfth century, the old Anglo-Saxon Coronation Service was submitted to revision. In one respect, the revision was designed to adjust the Service to contemporary conceptions of the royal authority. After the King had made his Promise, clergy and people were now required to declare their willingness to subject themselves to 'so excellent a Prince and Governor', and to render obedience to his commands. For the rest, the revision brought the Service into line with continental developments. All but the most important of the old prayers were replaced by new, drawn from a German source. Anointings of the King's hands, breast, shoulders and elbows were introduced before the anointing of his head. All these anointings were performed with the 'holy oil', the first of the oils used in the rite of Baptism and at ordinations of priests and bishops, and the only oil used hitherto at coronations. A second anointing of the head was now prescribed, this time with chrism, the second of the oils used at Baptism and at ordinations of priests and bishops. To the investitures, also, were now added the delivery of the 'Armills', or Bracelets, and clothing with the square-shaped imperial 'Pall' or Robe, each delivery being accompanied by an appropriate address. After the benediction, the King was first kissed by the bishops as a sign of their fealty to him, and then conducted to his throne by them to the singing of *Te Deum*.[1]

It was not until the fourteenth century that the mediaeval English Coronation rite reached its definitive form. At the accession of Edward II a new Oath was required (see below, p. 24), and circumstances in general suggested a further revision of the Service. The Service of the fourteenth century is known to us through a copy of *Liber Regalis* or 'the Royal Book', which was probably written at the instance of Nicholas Lytlington, Abbot of Westminster from 1362 to 1388, with the intention of codifying English Coronation procedure for all time, and which continues to be preserved at Westminster Abbey. *Liber Regalis* is also contained in the Missal[2] written for Lytlington, and likewise still at Westminster.

*Liber Regalis* is more than a Service-book. It collects in complete form all the elements of the Coronation tradition from the King's procession from the Tower of London through the City to the Royal Palace of Westminster, on the day before the Service, to the banquet which follows it. Of these elements one deserves particular notice. On the morning of the appointed day, there is an assemblage of nobles in Westminster Hall 'to consider about the consecration and election of the new King', and the King is then lifted into a throne specially prepared for him in the Hall. Dr Schramm has described this ceremony 'as a kind of secular enthronement at the hands of the Estates corresponding to that which took place at the end of the Coronation Service in the church'.[3] Only when this has been accomplished do the bishops, with the Abbot and monks of Westminster, come to Westminster Hall to conduct the King in solemn procession to the church for his Coronation.

[1] The text of the twelfth-century Service will be found in H. A. Wilson, *The Pontifical of Magdalen College*, Henry Bradshaw Society, 1910, pp. 89–95.
[2] Ed. by J. Wickham Legg, *Missale ad usum Ecclesiae Westmonasteriensis*, 3 vols., 1891, 1893 and 1896. *Lib. Reg.* is contained in vol. II, cols. 673–725.
[3] *History of the English Coronation*, p. 171.

The Service itself is much lengthened. The election by the bishops and people has become the Recognition. The King is to make an oblation of gold before taking the Oath. *Veni, Creator Spiritus* is introduced before the consecration and anointing of the King. An anointing between the shoulders is added to the others. Blessings are provided for the Sword, the Ring and the Crown. The Homage is introduced after the Inthronization. These are but a few of the additions of the fourteenth-century revision. The reviser was a man of historical sense. He restored a number of the prayers and forms of the '*Edgar*' Service, including the anthems 'Zadok the Priest' and 'Be strong and of a good courage', which had been omitted in the twelfth century. His direction for the putting on of the *Colobium sindonis*, the *Supertunica*, the Buskins and the Spurs was a recognition of established procedure. In other respects, also, he appears to have been admitting procedure which had become traditional, though it had been ignored in the rubrics of the earlier Service-books. The reviser had certainly spared himself no pains in discharging his task. He had consulted and borrowed from continental Coronation-books, in particular the French. Yet the character of his work is unmistakably English. He preserves the continuity of the English Coronation tradition; and his Service, though intricate and elaborate in detail, is logical in the sequence of its parts. It is a rite of great splendour and impressiveness, well worthy to replace its predecessors and to be the final English 'Order according to which the King must be crowned and anointed'.

### V. *LIBER REGALIS* ANGLICIZED. THE ORIGINS OF THE MODERN SERVICE, 1685 AND 1689

Queen Elizabeth I was the last English Sovereign whose Coronation Service was in Latin. The rite of *Liber Regalis* was used for her, as it had been used for her sister, Mary I. The fact that these two Sovereigns were Queens required no alteration of the rite. One ceremony alone had to be omitted: the Spurs were not put upon their heels. For the rest, all was done as for a King. For James I, an English version of the Latin Service was made; it 'had been drawn in haste', according to Heylin, 'and wanted many things which might have been considered in a time of leisure'.[1] These defects were remedied in 1626 for the coronation of Charles I. 'I had a perfect book of the Ceremonies of the Coronation made ready, agreeing in all things with *Liber Regalis*', notes Laud in his Diary. The Service of Charles I was used again for Charles II in 1661; it is the classical English version of the mediaeval rite.[2] With the exception that the Communion Service of the Prayer Book was substituted for the Mass, and that the functions of the Abbot of Westminster were performed by the Dean, the Prebendaries taking the places of the monks, the changes of the Reformation made little difference to the fourteenth-century tradition.

The accession of Charles II's successor in 1685 opens the modern chapter in the history of the English Coronation. As a Roman Catholic, James II could have no sincere regard for a ceremony conducted by Anglican bishops. Further, he was unable to receive Holy Communion from Anglican hands, and he was unwilling to be present at the Anglican Communion Service. Accordingly, when he gave Archbishop Sancroft instructions concerning his Coronation, he bade him 'leave out the Communion Service', and directed him to abridge the Coronation Rite as far as possible, though without destroying the essentials. James's instructions were all too faithfully obeyed. Not only abridgement, but mutilation, disturbance of arrangement, and unnecessary alteration were the characteristics of the work of Sancroft and his assistants. The form used at the anointing of the hands was transferred to the anointing of the head. The blessings of the royal ornaments were transformed into blessings of the King who was to wear them, since Sancroft appears to have disliked the blessing of objects. The forms recited at the delivery of the ornaments were changed. The Orb, which, though reckoned as belonging to the *Regalia*, had not hitherto been delivered to the Sovereign in the course of the Service, was now given at the same time as the Robe, and the address for the

---

[1] *Cyprianus Anglicus*, 1671, p. 145.

[2] For the text, see *The Coronation of King Charles I, 1626*, ed. with Introduction, etc., by Chr. Wordsworth, Henry Bradshaw Society, 1892; and L. J. Wickham Legg, *English Coronation Records*, pp. 245–71. Mr Wickham Legg's book facilitates comparison between *Liber Regalis* and the Service of 1626.

Robe was made to include the Orb. As the Orb was not an alternative to the Sceptre with the Cross, it had to be taken away as soon as it was given. These are but a few instances of Sancroft's methods. His Service needs to be studied in detail for the extent of his vandalism to be appreciated. Yet it must be recognized that Sancroft did not destroy the ancient pattern of the rite.[1]

The 'Glorious Revolution', with which James II's brief and troubled reign came to an end in 1689, and the accession of William and Mary as co-Sovereigns, inevitably opened questions concerning the Coronation Service. For one thing, there was a plain need for a revised Coronation Oath, free of the ambiguities of which James had taken advantage. For another, it had to be considered whether there should be a return to the Service of 1661, or a further revision made. An Act of Parliament established a new Oath (see below, p. 28). In respect to the Service, decision was in favour of a revision. The Coronation Service of 1689 was the work of Henry Compton, Bishop of London, who, as Sancroft refused to take the oath to the new Sovereigns, had to discharge the Archbishop's function at the Coronation. Compton had no liturgical learning, and was given four weeks in which to make his revision. It is not astonishing, therefore, that he proved no less destructive than Sancroft, whose Service he took as the material on which to work. Nevertheless, in one important respect Compton reverted to an ancient model. He inserted the greater part of the Coronation Order into the Communion Service, placing it in between the Sermon and the Offertory. It is improbable that in doing this he was guided by the precedent of the *Pontifical of Egbert*. It is more likely that, out of a deliberate design to prevent a repetition of James II's separation of Coronation from Communion, he adopted the arrangement of the Service for the Consecration of Bishops contained in the Book of Common Prayer.

Compton perpetuated Sancroft's mistakes and mutilations, and made many more. Ignoring the logical and historical connexion between the Oath and the Recognition, he widely separated them,

[1] For Sancroft's Service, see L. J. Wickham Legg, *English Coronation Records*, pp. 288–316.

leaving the Recognition at the beginning (it could have no other place), and inserting the Oath between the Sermon and the Anointing. The Anointing itself was severely pruned. The ancient prayer for the bestowal of the virtues requisite in good rulers which was derived from '*Egbert*', and which Sancroft had been content to abridge, was jettisoned. The 'Consecration' of the Sovereigns, which followed it, was deprived of its Preface form, and much mutilated. A petition for the blessing of the oil was also now introduced into it. Perhaps it should be set down to Compton's credit that the notion of the consecration of the Sovereigns was not allowed to disappear. With some reason, Compton reduced the number of the anointings to three, viz. on the hands, the breast and the head; but he unnecessarily inverted the ancient order, so that the head was anointed first. He further altered the traditional order at the investitures; the putting on of the Crown now came last. After the crowning, he introduced a new feature, viz. the Presentation of the Bible, which was accompanied by a long address adducing Old Testament precedent. Almost all the addresses of delivery in Compton's Service were greatly expanded, either by the addition of phrases borrowed from Scripture, or by turgid passages of his own composing. By this means alone, the length of the Service was considerably increased. At the Communion Service, the Proper was reduced. The Introit and Communion anthems were discontinued (the Gradual had disappeared in 1603). The old Proper Collect was replaced by the first of the two Collects for the Sovereign in the Communion Service. A new, and poor, Proper Preface was provided. It is a matter for surprise that the Collect at the Oblation of the Bread and Wine was permitted to remain with but little alteration. 'The general result of Compton's revision', it has been said by an eminent authority on English coronation rites, 'was that nothing of the ancient order remained in its place without change; and very little of it was left at all.'[1] On the other hand, the historic pattern was not obliterated. Enough of it was retained to preserve the identity of the rite as a Service of the Consecration and Crowning of English Sovereigns. In spite of Compton's disarrangement, disfigurement and mis-

[1] H. A. Wilson in 'The English Coronation Orders', *Journal of Theological Studies*, July 1901.

understanding of his material, there is still to be discerned in his work the august tradition of *Liber Regalis*.[1]

Compton's rite for William and Mary has been followed at the Coronations of their successors, not, however, *verbatim et litteratim*. There have been modifications of phraseology, and a gradual and progressive abbreviation of the longer prayers and addresses of delivery. By the time of Queen Victoria's Coronation, in 1838, a marked shortening is noticeable. By 1838 also the ancient ceremonial context of the Service had disappeared. The procession from the Tower of London to Westminster had been discontinued by James II, and had not been revived by his successors. The assembly of peers in Westminster Hall on the morning of Coronation Day, the placing of the Sovereign in his seat, and the procession from the Hall to the Abbey for the Service, together with the Coronation Banquet at which the officers of the Royal Household performed their several services as Steward, Butler, Naperer, etc., when the Service had ended, continued up to the Coronation of George IV in 1821. This Coronation, 'though the most gorgeous pageant ever exhibited in England, excited far less enthusiasm in the public generally, than that of any of his predecessors',[2] according to a contemporary observer. The personal unpopularity of George IV, combined with disapproval at the extravagance of the Banquet, brought discredit upon 'the gorgeous pageant', the religious character of which seems hardly to have been recognized. When William IV succeeded his brother in 1830, the public mind was hostile to any but the lowest expenditure on a Coronation. There was also a feeling that such a ceremony was at variance with the spirit of the age. The editor of *The Times* would have abridged a great part of the Service as being 'compounded of the worst dregs of popery and feudalism'.[3] Nevertheless, there was a widespread desire to retain the procession from Westminster Hall to the Abbey. Two months before his Coronation, in *The London Gazette* of 10 July 1831, the King declared 'his commands

[1] For the text of Compton's Service, see L. G. Wickham Legg, *English Coronation Records*, pp. 317–42.

[2] *Chapters on Coronations*, 1838, p. 197. The author is supposed to have been W. C. Taylor.

[3] Quoted from *The Gentleman's Magazine*, 1 Sept. 1831.

that no ceremonies are to be celebrated at the Coronation, except the sacred rites attending the administration of the royal oath in Westminster Abbey. The usual procession and feast are to be dispensed with.' To serve some part of the function of Westminster Hall, a retiring room, or 'Annexe', was erected at the west door of the Abbey. Here the *Regalia*, brought in procession by the clergy of the Abbey, were delivered to the Lords who were to carry them; and from the Annexe the royal procession moved into the church. The arrangements of 1831 were meagre in comparison with the splendours of the past; but they preserved the essential ceremony, the Coronation Service itself, without abridgement of the kind desired by the editor of *The Times*. In 1838, there was no question of dispensing with 'the sacred rites attending the administration of the royal oath', as William IV's command had strangely described the substantive ceremonies of Anointing and Investiture, to which the Oath is preliminary. The new arrangements made the Coronation of William IV the shortest on record in several hundred years. The arrangements of 1831 were repeated at the Coronation of Queen Victoria. They have been repeated at each subsequent Coronation; and they will be followed again in 1953. No one would desire a revival of the Banquet; yet it may be permitted to express a hope that the assembly in Westminster Hall and the procession from the Hall to the Abbey are only in abeyance.

## VI. CORONATIONS IN THE TWENTIETH CENTURY. THE CORONATION SERVICE OF QUEEN ELIZABETH II

The Coronation of 1838 was the last of its century. Sixty-four years later, when the Coronation of King Edward VII was planned for 26 June 1902, all the circumstances of a new age, together with general rejoicing at the ending of the South African war, combined to give to the ceremony a new significance and a peculiar solemnity. Almost on the eve of the appointed day, the ceremony was postponed *sine die* on account of the King's sudden illness. When it was eventually performed on 9 August, it gained rather than lost in brilliance and meaning, in spite of the absence of the foreign delegations which, with one exception, had returned home after the King's illness had been announced. Representatives from the Dominions, Colonies, Dependencies and Protectorates were present in a vast multitude. The contingents were composed not only of British officials, but also of the native peoples; and the muster was as impressive as at the Diamond Jubilee in 1897. If the Coronation of King Edward VII was not the international event which at first it had promised to be, it was instead, as Lord Rosebery said of it, 'something of a family festival of the British Empire'. This newly acquired character was maintained at the Coronations of King George V and King George VI.

In several respects the Coronations of the twentieth century have exhibited a notable improvement upon those of the nineteenth. For one thing, the manner of performing the Service has been consonant with its sacred character and solemn language. No longer is it possible to describe the rite as 'a pageant', or to regard it as a court mime or a picturesque old English custom. It has become again what St Dunstan designed it to be, the 'Consecration' of the Sovereign. The measure of this recovery may be gauged by a passage from a leading article in *The Times*, entitled 'The Lord's Anointed', on the Coronation of King George VI:[1] 'As the golden canopy was held over King Edward's chair, and the Archbishop went in under it to the King, bearing the consecrated oil, as into a tabernacle, it seemed that these two men were alone with God, performing an act greater than they knew, more solemn than any person present could hope to understand.' Again, careful preparation and rehearsal have avoided the confusion and consequent loss of dignity which marred the Coronation of Queen Victoria; 'Pray tell me what I am to do', the Queen was compelled to ask of the Dean of Westminster, 'for they don't know.'[2] Also, and by no means least important, those responsible for the text and general arrangement of the Service have had a better understanding of its meaning, its history, and the numerous traditions associated with it, than at any time in the last three hundred years. Many, though not all, of the ravages wrought by Compton have been repaired. The Oath is once more attached to the Recognition, to which it logically belongs.

[1] *The Times*, 13 May 1937.
[2] C. C. F. Greville, *A Journal of the Reign of Queen Victoria*, 1885, vol. I, p. 106.

Older forms of prayer and address have been restored, not primarily on account of their antiquity, but because in simplicity and directness of expression, they are more suited to their purpose than were the pompous compositions of 1689. The Communion Service, also, has been embellished by the replacement of the traditional Proper Introit and Offertory anthems, and by the provision of a Proper Collect.

In the Form and Order of the Service drawn up for the Coronation of Queen Elizabeth II the process of revision has been continued, by way partly of rearrangement, partly of the restoration of a significant traditional ornament, partly of the introduction of new features, and partly of simplification in the phraseology both of prayers and rubrics. The chief of these changes deserve particular notice.

From 1689 to 1937 the *Presentation of the Holy Bible* was made after the Putting on of the Crown. For all Compton's address appealing to the precedents of the Deuteronomic King and of King Jehoash, this arrangement was awkward, and incongruous. The Bible does not belong to the *Regalia*. In course of time, the Hebrew analogy lost its persuasiveness; by 1838 reference to it had been omitted, and in 1902 the address was reduced to a few sentences. The new position of the 'Presenting' of the Bible, now numbered *V*, and the revised address accompanying it make the ceremony follow appropriately upon the Oath, in which the Queen undertakes to 'maintain the Laws of God' and 'the true profession of the Gospel'. The assistance of the Moderator of the General Assembly of the Church of Scotland in the act of presentation is a new feature. In the form of the oath settled in 1937, the Queen swears to 'maintain in the *United Kingdom* the Protestant Reformed Religion established by law'. It is eminently appropriate, therefore, that at this moment the principal minister of the Scottish Establishment should be associated with the principal ecclesiastic of the English.

The prayer which follows the hymn, 'Come, Holy Ghost, our souls inspire', under the title, *VII. The Anointing*, and which represents the historic 'consecration' of the Sovereign, has recovered both the ancient and appropriate phrase, 'the exalter of the humble and the strength of thy chosen', in its opening

20

address, and also the traditional ending, 'through Jesus Christ our Lord', which Compton had omitted.

The division numbered *IX*, and entitled *The Investing with the Armills, the Stole Royal and the Robe Royal: and the Delivery of the Orb* is the result of complete revision and re-arrangement and includes an ornament restored after a long period of disuse. In 1911 and 1937, the equivalent division was entitled *The Investing with the Armill and Royal Robe, and the Delivery of the Orb*. In this context, the word 'Armill', in the singular, designates the stole-like strip of embroidered silk worn beneath the Royal Robe. In the new title, 'Armills', in the plural, is employed in its original sense of 'Bracelets'. The use of the Bracelets, or Armills, has been revived. The address recited at the moment of investiture combines a version of that used in the twelfth century (when the Bracelets first found a place among the Investitures) with a modern clause interpreting the ornaments as symbols of the bond which unites the Queen with her Peoples. The singular 'Armill' of the previous title is now named the 'Stole Royal'. Like the *Colobium sindonis* and *Supertunica* it is put upon the Queen without an address. A newly introduced sub-heading now disconnects the Delivery of the Orb from the Investing with the Robe; and the respective symbolisms of these ornaments are expressed in separate addresses, in place of the single address, introduced by Sancroft in 1685 and enlarged by Compton in 1689. Although this re-arrangement will not satisfy all the historians of the Coronation, it goes a considerable way towards disentangling the confusion of the seventeenth century.

Revision, though to a smaller extent, is apparent in the next four divisions. The expanded title of *X. The Investiture per Annulum, et per Sceptrum et Baculum* is complete for the first time since 1685. Sancroft, the author of the title, omitted reference to the Sceptre, and Compton perpetuated the title without completing it. The address at the giving of the Ring has been brought into closer agreement with the form contained in *Liber Regalis* and in the rite of the twelfth century. The brief sentences recited at the delivery of Sceptre and Rod are succeeded by a short address expressing the duties symbolized separately by the two ornaments. The prayer to be said before *The Putting on of the Crown (XI)* is a re-writing of the previous form; the blessing of the Crown follows the precedent of *Liber Regalis* and the twelfth century. *The Benediction* (*XII*) recovers the larger structure given to it by Sancroft and Compton, and modified in 1902. The second clause has been rewritten; it is better suited to the changed conditions of the Commonwealth, and of the British communities at home and overseas, than the equivalent clause in earlier forms of the Benediction. The charge, 'Stand firm, and hold fast from henceforth the seat', etc., in *XIII*. *The Inthroning*, has been abridged by the removal of the bishops' petition for a continuance of the royal favour towards them. The reasons for which the petition was included in the first Coronation Service of 973 no longer exist. The charge has gained in effectiveness by the removal, and also by the omission of a reference (in a quotation from Psalm lxxxix. 37) to the sun, infelicitously added by Sancroft to the final phrase.

The Communion Service has been enriched by the restoration of an anthem for the *Gradual* and Alleluia; the anthem is borrowed from the Gradual of *Liber Regalis*. In place of the Offertory anthem, 'the people shall with one voice sing' the hymn, 'All people that on earth do dwell'. This is the first appearance, in the long history of the English Coronation rite, of a congregational hymn. Another new feature is introduced after the Queen's Oblations. Provision is made for a special prayer for, and blessing of, the Queen's Consort, the Duke of Edinburgh. Queen Anne is the one English Queen to have been married at the time of her Coronation; the presence of her Consort, Prince George of Denmark, was recognized only in his precedence at the Homage. The *Proper Preface* is mainly a new composition; it contains an echo of the Proper Preface of 1838 and, it may be added, of the Royal Style. The singing of an anthem at Communion time has been revived. There is a new, and seemly, departure from previous usage after the administration of the Sacrament. The Queen returns from the Altar, not to the Throne, but to her faldstool. Her return to the Throne is delayed until the Post-Communion Prayer is ended. Then, resuming the Crown, the Sceptre and the Rod, she proceeds to the Throne for *Gloria in excelsis Deo*, and there remains for the rest of the Service. The singing of two verses of 'The National Anthem' during the Queen's progress from St Edward's Chapel to the west door of the Church, at the end of the Service, is also an innovation.

Very few of these changes can fail to win general approbation. They neither alter nor weaken the authentic character of the Service. How closely related to the classical English Coronation rite the modern Service, in its latest revision, continues to be, may be seen from a comparison of it with the rubrical directions of *Liber Regalis* (see Appendix, p. 67f.). Where the changes of 1953 are without precedent, they are nevertheless in harmony with the nature and history of the rite, and are proof of the enduring vitality of its tradition.

The tradition of the English Coronation is not rigid and immutable like that of a Byzantine Imperial ceremony; without losing its individuality, it can adapt itself, or its parts, to new conditions with such signal success that we may not inaptly say of it, *Plus ça change, plus c'est la même chose.* Borrowing from biblical, Frankish, Roman, Byzantine, German and French sources, arranging and re-arranging these diverse elements from period to period, and adding to them from its own native inspiration, it has presented them, and still presents them to us in a remarkable unity, which is distinctively English in aspect. The Coronation Service is a mirror, as no other English institution can be, of the historical process in which our ancestors have lived, in which our nation has been formed, and in which we ourselves are living to-day. It reflects the persistent English intertwining of sacred and secular, of civil and ecclesiastical. It reflects particularly the historic English conception of the mutual relations of Sovereign, Church and People, and of all three to God, Whose blessing and protection it invokes. In a word, the English Coronation Service symbolizes national continuity considered *sub specie Christianitatis.*

At her Coronation Service in 1953, Queen Elizabeth II will be anointed as her ancestor Edgar, first King of All England, was anointed at the first English Coronation Service in 973. She will receive, as from God, the ensigns of royalty, as Edgar received them. She will be blessed, as Edgar was blessed. She will be set, as Edgar was set, in the Throne of the Realm as a Christian Sovereign, holding her dignity by the grace and 'by the authority of Almighty God'.

In England, an oath at the beginning of the King's inauguration has been customary since the tenth century. Its history and tenor are of some importance. In the two earlier drafts of St Dunstan's Coronation Service, the King is described as enjoining a 'Mandate', consisting of three 'Precepts', upon himself and his people, after his inthronization or at the end of Mass. The terms of the Mandate are possibly older than Dunstan's time. At the Coronation of 973, the Mandate and its Precepts were transformed into a threefold Promise, binding the King alone, and now to be recited after his election by the bishops and people and before his anointing, a position in the Service suggested by West Frankish usage. The Promise recited by Edgar was as follows:

These three things I promise in Christ's name to the Christian People subject to me: First, that the Church of God and the whole Christian People shall have true peace at all time by our judgement; Second, that I will forbid extortion and all kinds of wrong-doing to all orders of men; Third, that I will enjoin equity and mercy in all judgements, that God, Who is kind and merciful, may vouchsafe His mercy to me and to you.[1]

To this solemn Promise, all are directed by the rubric to respond, 'Amen'.

With slight verbal changes, the Promise of 973 remained in use to the Coronation of Edward I in 1274. For some time before that, however, it had ceased to correspond with the realities of developing English political conditions. It was no effective safeguard against disregard of inherited law and custom on the part of the Sovereign; and it presented no barrier against an unlimited extension of the royal executive power. The dispute between the King and the barons, with which the reign of Edward II began, led to a profound change in regard to the Promise. As the price of his Coronation, Edward II was compelled to make concessions to the barons in an Oath, new in form and partly in content, and superseding the ancient Promise. The new Oath consisted of interrogations and answers, four in number; the form was modelled

[1] For the original Latin see L. G. Wickham Legg, *English Coronation Records*, p. 15.

upon a German oath of the tenth century, which in turn had been suggested by the questions put to, and the answers given by, a bishop at or before his consecration.[1] The first of the four questions committed the King to guaranteeing existing laws. The fourth question was a novelty, destined to be of utmost importance for the future. It bound the King to 'grant to be held and observed the just laws and customs that the community (*la communaute*) of your realm shall determine' and to 'defend and strengthen them to the honour of God'.[2] The new Oath was therefore a constitutional document, which (to quote Professor B. Wilkinson) 'both extended the political interest of the community and challenged the legislative ascendancy of the ruler'.[3] Edward II's Oath was sworn in French. *Liber Regalis* and Abbot Lytlington's Missal give us a Latin version of the Oath. Neither of these documents includes a version of the important fourth clause; but both allow for its introduction in the words, 'There shall be added those things that be right'.[4] On the other hand, both these documents introduce a question and answer which had no place in the Oath of Edward II. The purpose of this further interrogation, which derived its origin and some of its phraseology ultimately from the West Frankish Coronation Oath, was to confirm and secure the rights, privileges and interests of the Church. In its full and final form, therefore, the mediaeval Coronation Oath consisted of five interrogations and answers, of which the specifically ecclesiastical was the last. The English version used for Henry VII is given in the *Little Device* for his Coronation as follows:

'Will ye graunt and keepe to the people of Englande the Lawes and customes to them as olde rightfull and devoute Kinges graunted, and the same ratifie, and confirme by yo^r othe? And specially lawes customes and Liberties graunted to the Clergie, and people by your Predecessors, and glorious King Saynct Edwarde?' *Answer*, 'I graunt and promit.' 'Ye shall keepe after your strenght and power

---

[1] Questions and answers of this kind are still to be found in the Service for consecrating Archbishops and Bishops in the Ordinal of the Prayer Book.

[2] B. Wilkinson, *Constitutional History of Mediaeval England 1216–1399*, vol. II, 'Politics and the Constitution 1307–1399', 1952, p. 108. Chapter 1 of this book, 'The Coronation of Edward II', is the most recent and authoritative discussion of this subject.

[3] *Op. cit.* p. 12.      [4] See p. 72 below.

the church of God to the Clergie. And the people hoole peace and godly concord.' *Answer*, 'I shall keepe.' 'Ye shall make to be done after your strenght and power rightfull Justice in all your domes and judgementes, and discrecion wt. mercie and trowthe.' *Answer*, 'I shall do.' 'Do ye graunte the rightfull Lawes and customs to be holden and promitte yow after your strenght and power such lawes as to the worship of God shalbe chosen by your people by yow to be strenghthenid and defended?' *Answer*, 'I graunte and promitte.' 'Domine Rex, Sir King. We aske of yow to be perfectly geven and graunted unto us, that ye shall keepe to us, and eche of us the Privileges of the Lawe Canone and of holie church and dewe Lawes and right-fulnes, and us and them defende as a devout and christian King ought to do. And in Likewise to do and graunte throughout all yor Realme to every busshop and to all the churches to them committed.' *Answer*, 'With good will and devowt soule I promit, and perfectly graunte, that to yow and every of yow and all the churches to yow committed, I shall keepe the privileges of Lawe Canon and of the holie church, and dewe Lawe and rightfulnes. And I shall in asmoch as I may by reason and right, by gods grace defende yow and every of yow throughout my Realme, and all the churches to yow committed. All these things and every of them I Henry King of England promit and confirme, so helpe me god, and by thes holie Evangelistes by me bodily towched upon this holie aulter.'[1]

It is obvious that the terms of the mediaeval Oath were at variance with the conceptions of Kingship entertained by Henry VIII and the remaining Tudors. For his own Coronation, Henry VIII at first proposed to bring into use what he may have believed to be a form of Oath older than that of Edward II, but what in fact appears to be a composition of later date.[2] Although this form stresses the royal dignity, its terms were not strong enough for Henry; and in the event, no change was made in the traditional Oath at the Coronation of 1509. It is possible, however, that Henry had in mind to bequeath to his successors an Oath so phrased as clearly to express his own conception of the royal authority. Among the Cotton MSS. in the British Museum is one exhibiting Henry's revision, in his own hand, of the supposedly

[1] L. G. Wickham Legg, *English Coronation Records*, pp. 230 ff.
[2] For the text, see L. G. Wickham Legg, *op. cit.*, pp. 240 f.; see also P. E. Schramm, *History of the English Coronation*, p. 215.

older form which he had considered and rejected before his Coronation. Had this revised Oath been adopted, it would formally have swept away those safeguards against royal absolutism which the mediaeval Oath was designed to erect: the King was to swear that he

shall kepe and mayntene the lawfull right and libertees of old tyme graunted by the rightuous Cristen kinges of Englond to the holy chirche of ingland nott preiudyciall to hys Jurysdiccion and dignite ryall...and the rightes of the Crowne hurte decayed or lost to his power shall call again into the auncyent astate...and that he shall graunte to hold lawes and approvyd customes of the realme and lawfull and not prejudiciall to hys crowne or Imperiall Juris[diction] to his power kepe them and affirme them which the noblys and people have made and chosen wt his consent.[1]

Henry VIII's Oath was never introduced into the Coronation Service. For Edward VI, the traditional Oath was adjusted to Tudor ideas by some alterations of phraseology; by the omission of the clause securing the rights of the Church; and by a complete change in the fourth interrogation, whereby the initiation of legislation is taken to be the King's, and the people's right is limited to consent. To this extent was the constitutional movement of the mediaeval period reversed. It is not known what form of Oath was taken by Mary I and Elizabeth I.

The Stewart view of royal authority was little different from that of Henry VIII; and it was one of the charges against Archbishop Laud that, to suit this view, he had altered the traditional Oath, when, as Bishop of St David's and Vice-Dean of Westminster, he had drawn up the Coronation Service of Charles I. He was accused of omitting reference to the people from the promise to confirm the Laws granted to clergy and people by St Edward, and also of removing mention of the people's choice of the Laws and Customs which the King was asked to defend. He was further accused of introducing the reservation 'agreeing to the prerogative of the Kings' into the promise to confirm the Laws.[2] Laud's defence was that he found no mention of the

---

[1] Wickham Legg, *op. cit.*, pp. 240 f.

[2] For Charles I's Oath see Chr. Wordsworth, *The Coronation of King Charles I, 1626*, Henry Bradshaw Society, 1892, pp. 18 ff.

people choosing laws in the Oath of James I, and that he knew nothing about the other two points.

The interpretation put upon the Oath by James II led, as we have noted above, to a remodelling of it by Act of Parliament in 1689. The intention of Parliament in enacting the new Oath is expressed in the preamble to the Act, here quoted:

Whereas by the Law and ancient Usage of this Realm, the Kings and Queens thereof have taken a Solemn Oath upon the Evangelists at their respective Coronations, to maintain the Statutes Laws and Customs of the said Realm, and all the People and Inhabitants thereof, in their Spiritual and Civil Rights and Properties: But forasmuch as the Oath itself on such occasion administered, hath heretofore been framed in doubtful Words and Expressions, with relation to ancient Laws and Constitutions at this time unknown: To the end therefore that one uniform Oath may be in all times to come taken by the Kings and Queens of this Realm, and to them respectively administred at the times of their and every of their Coronation: May it please your Majesties that it be enacted,[1] etc.

The Parliamentary character of the English monarchy was decisively settled by the Oath of 1689. The modification made by the Act of Union, 1707, involved no alteration in the structure or tenor of the Oath.

For the Coronation of King George VI, the first question of the Oath was so amended as to accord with the Commonwealth settlement sanctioned by the Statute of Westminster, and the reference to Parliament was omitted. In the third question, a reference to the United Kingdom was introduced in connexion with the promise to maintain 'the Protestant Reformed Religion established by law'. These amendments received the authority, not of Parliament, but of the Privy Council only.

### VIII. THE ANOINTING. ITS INTERPRETATION

The parallel drawn between the coronation of Kings and the consecration of bishops has already been noticed. With the universal adoption, in the West, of the practice of anointing at the

[1] *Statutes at Large*, 1735, vol. III, p. 19.

consecration of bishops, it was inevitable that sooner or later the anointing of the King should be explained in sacramental terms suggested by the sacramental anointing of the bishop. St Peter Damiani, Cardinal Bishop of Ostia, who died in 1071, reckoned 'the anointing of the King' to be the fifth of the twelve Sacraments of the Church. In this line of tradition, an unnamed Norman writer, known as the Anonymous of York, claimed for the King, in virtue of his anointing, the position of Supreme Ruler over the Church, and attributed to him the office of Christ in granting remission to sinners and reconciliation to penitents.

The claim is extreme; and already when the Anonymous wrote, in the days of William II and St Anselm, it was rather old-fashioned. Some historians have been led to suppose that it caused the abandonment of the use of chrism in the Coronation Service of the twelfth century, chrism being the most sacred of the oils, employed both at Confirmation and ordinations. The evidence of the English liturgical MSS. of the period, however, does not support this view. Whereas the MSS. of the Anglo-Saxon Coronation Service do not refer to chrism, the English MSS. of the twelfth-century Service direct its use. The use of chrism was introduced into the English Coronation with that Service, how-ever the matter may have been treated on the Continent. Indeed, if chrism had not been used, the answer which Grosseteste made to Henry III's question, 'How does the Sacrament of anointing increase the royal dignity?', would be without point.

Grosseteste answers that the Sacrament of anointing is 'a sign of the privilege of receiving the sevenfold gift of the most holy Spirit'. It is comparable, that is to say, with Confirmation. It imposes upon the King the duty of making 'all the acts of his rule to be worthy of admiration in divine and heroic virtues'. Grosseteste adds that the anointing confers no sacerdotal status. Grosseteste was, of course, a Canonist, and gave a Canonist's answer to Henry's question. Yet, if a contrary position had been generally held, and no doubt about the matter had been felt, Henry would have had no reason to put his question. When the settlement of the familiar Seven Sacraments was accepted as final, there could be no further place for a Sacrament of royal anointing. In a letter to Edward II, dealing with a legendary gift of an ampulla of 'most holy anointing' to St Thomas of Canterbury by the Blessed Virgin, Pope John XXII stated that 'the royal anointing impresses nothing upon the soul',[1] as certain Sacraments are said to do. The Pope's statement is dictated by the prevailing theology.

In the end, the English Canonists admitted that certain persons, i.e. the Common Lawyers, held the Sovereign to be, in virtue of the anointing, not a mere layman, but a *persona mixta cum sacerdote*. The Common Lawyers, on their side, did not press this view to its strictest theological conclusions. The view had a practical value in enabling the Common Lawyers to resist ecclesiastical encroachment, when they wished to do so. Bracton, while he regards the King as 'God's Vicar', asserts a 'large difference' between priesthood and kingship, which enables him to state that their jurisdictions are delimited and distinct, except that the two swords, civil and ecclesiastical, ought to assist each other.[2]

The mediaeval controversy concerning the effect of the anointing upon the Sovereign is no longer a live issue. By the Act of Supremacy of 1559, jurisdiction over the English Estate Ecclesiastical and Spiritual is perpetually annexed to the Crown. The Queen is 'over all persons and in all causes, as well ecclesiastical as civil, within her dominions, supreme'. On the other hand, the 'chief power', as Article 37 states, does not give to our Sovereigns 'the ministering either of God's Word or of the Sacraments'. The Sovereign is not a clerical or ecclesiastical personage.

How, then, it may be asked is the anointing to be interpreted in our time? The Coronation Service itself suggests the answer. The anointing is a sacred act having biblical warrant. It is not a Sacrament, in the later, restricted sense of the term. Yet we may not improperly describe it, in the opening words of Article 25, 'Of the Sacraments', as a 'sign of grace and God's good will' towards the Anointed; and we may recall St Augustine's description of Sacraments in general as being 'certain, as it were, visible words'.[3] The act of anointing is, as it were, 'a visible word',

---

[1] The texts, with translations, of Grosseteste's and John XXII's letters will be found in L. G. Wickham Legg, *English Coronation Records*, pp. 66–76.

[2] See Bracton, *De legibus et consuetudinibus*, De actionibus viii, 5, ed. Sir Travers Twiss, Rolls Series, vol. lxx, p. 170.

[3] *Contra Faustum* xix, 16.

uttering a special blessing upon a dedicated life, promising those gifts of the Spirit, for which prayer is made immediately before the act is performed, and pronouncing 'consecration' to the office and work of a Christian Sovereign.

## IX. THE CORONATION VESTURE

After the Anointing, the royal vesture is put upon the Queen. This consists of the *Colobium sindonis*, the *Supertunica*, the Armills, the Royal Stole and the Royal Robe.

*Colobium sindonis* means 'muslin undergarment'. In its ancient form it had either short sleeves or no sleeves at all. As a Coronation garment, it represents the *tunica* of the ancient world common to both sexes and to all classes of society. Civilians, clergy and women wore it as *talaris*, i.e. reaching to the ankles, and with sleeves. It survives among us in this long form as the ecclesiastical vestments known as 'alb' and 'rochet'. Soldiers, their officers and workmen wore it cut off at the knee. The well-known mosaics of the Emperor Justinian and the Empress Theodora in the church of S. Vitale at Ravenna show it in both these forms. On civil occasions, the Byzantine emperors wore the tunic at ankle length. English Sovereigns wear it similarly at their Coronations. Since the time of James II it has reverted to the sleeveless form.

The *Supertunica*, sometimes called *Dalmatica*, is worn, as its name indicates, over the tunica or *Colobium*, and is made of cloth of gold. It is identical in origin with the embroidered church vestment worn by deacons over the alb and known as a 'dalmatic'. Both the royal and ecclesiastical garments derive their origin from the richly decorated over-tunic, or *tunica-palmata*, worn on ceremonial occasions by consuls under the Empire, and later a distinctive Byzantine imperial dress. The Queen wears the *Supertunica*, as the emperor wore it, belted with a rich girdle.

The word 'Armills' is derived from the Latin *armillae*, meaning 'bracelets'. They are probably of Teutonic derivation, and formed a part of military equipment. *Liber Regalis* applies the term to a piece of silk worn stole-wise round the neck and tied to the arms. This seems to be the result of confusion. The Byzantine emperors used to wear, over the *Supertunica*, a garment designated the *loros*, a long embroidered and jewelled scarf, which originated in the folded *toga picta* of the consuls. The Norman Kings of Sicily adopted the Byzantine imperial costume; their example was imitated by others. Edward I was buried wearing a *loros*. How the *loros* came to be confused with the Armills, and how it came to be tied to the arms, cannot be said. The introduction of the Stole-armills did not drive out the Bracelet-armills at Coronation, however. Queen Elizabeth I wore them. But in 1661, we read of the 'Armilla of the fashion of a Stole made of Cloth of Gold', and nothing is said of 'Bracelets'. So the 'Armill' remained until 1937. In 1953 the confusion has been resolved. The 'Armills' are 'Bracelets' again. The stole-like '*loros*' is now named the 'Royal Stole'.

The Royal Robe, sometimes called 'the Imperial Mantle', is one of the oldest distinctive garments of the Byzantine emperors. Those who draw a parallel between the Sovereign's coronation and a bishop's consecration identify the Royal Robe with the ecclesiastical cope. The antecedent of the cope, however, is the raincoat of antiquity, whereas that of the Robe is the purple cloak of the *Imperator*. Moreover, unlike the cope, which is semicircular and fastened across the breast, the Robe should be square and fastened by a brooch on the right shoulder, as in the mosaic of Justinian. The Great Seals of Henry I, Stephen, Henry II and Edward I represent it as so worn, likewise the effigy of Henry III in Westminster Abbey. To use his left hand when wearing the Robe in this manner, the King had to fold it over his left arm. The inconvenience of so doing doubtless led the wearer to move the brooch to his breast, and to wear the Robe cope-wise, as it is worn to-day.

Two other articles of Byzantine imperial attire were formerly put on by English Sovereigns at their Coronation. These are the Buskins, or Hose, and the Sandals. They were worn up to the Coronation of James II; but were discontinued in 1689.

The coronation vesture was originally kept with the *Regalia* in Westminster Abbey. According to a Westminster legend, reported about 1450 by a monk of the monastery, 'St Edward King and Confessor, as a reminder to them that shall come and for the dignity of the royal coronation, caused to be preserved in this church all the royal ornaments with which he himself was crowned'. The legend has no basis in fact; but it records and is designed to explain a custom of long standing. It is on account of the Westminster prescriptive right in the matter that the Sovereign is clothed in the course of the Service not only with the symbolical Robe, but also with the lesser vesture, the *Colobium sindonis*, the *Supertunica*, and formerly the Sandals, all of which were traditionally 'St Edward's', kept, not in the Sovereign's Wardrobe, but in the Abbey. For the same reason, the vesture is removed and left in St Edward's Chapel, when the Service is ended.

The movement of the Coronation Service will be easily followed, if the following points are borne in mind:

(i) The people accept the Queen as Sovereign at THE RECOGNITION (III).

(ii) The Queen, in taking THE OATH, makes her solemn promise to govern by and to maintain the Laws of her Peoples (IV).

(iii) At THE ANOINTING, the Queen receives Consecration, or the grace of a special Divine Blessing, for her sovereign office and work (VII).

(iv) THE INVESTITURE with THE SWORD, THE ROYAL ROBE, THE SCEPTRE and ROD, etc., THE CROWNING, and THE INTHRONIZATION are the outward and visible signs of the Queen's assumption of her royal office (VIII–XI and XIII).

# THE FORM AND ORDER OF
# HER MAJESTY'S CORONATION

## I. THE PREPARATION

*In the morning upon the day of the Coronation early, care is to be taken that the Ampulla* [1] *be filled with the Oil for the anointing, and, together with the Spoon, be laid ready upon the Altar in the Abbey Church.*

*The Litany* [2] *shall be sung as the Dean and Prebendaries and the choir of Westminster proceed from the Altar to the west door of the Church.*

*The Archbishops being already vested in their Copes and Mitres and the Bishops Assistant in their Copes, the procession shall be formed immediately outside of the west door of the Church, and shall wait till notice be given of the approach of her Majesty, and shall then begin to move into the Church.*

*And the people shall remain standing from the Entrance until the beginning of the Communion Service.*

## II. THE ENTRANCE INTO THE CHURCH

*The Queen, as soon as she enters at the west door of the Church, is to be received with this Anthem* [3]:

Psalm cxxii. 1-3, 6, 7

I was glad when they said unto me, We will go into the house of the Lord. Our feet shall stand in thy gates, O Jerusalem. Jerusalem is built as a city that is at unity in itself. O pray for the peace of Jerusalem: they shall prosper that love thee. Peace be within thy walls, and plenteousness within thy palaces.

---

[1] *The Ampulla*, which contains the oil, is made in the form of an eagle with outstretched wings. It is thought that it may have belonged to the original *Regalia*, and have escaped destruction in 1649.

[2] *The Litany* was introduced into the Coronation Service in the twelfth century, and has occupied various positions in the Service. From 1689 to 1911 it was sung before the beginning of the Communion Service. It was moved to its present position in 1937.

[3] The use of Psalm cxxii as an anthem to be sung at *the Entrance into the Church* dates from the Coronation of Charles I in 1626.

*The Queen shall in the mean time pass up through the body of the Church, into and through the choir, and so up the stairs to the Theatre* [1] *and having passed by her Throne, she shall make her humble adoration, and then kneeling at the faldstool set for her before her Chair of Estate on the south side of the Altar, use some short private prayers; and after, sit down in her Chair.*

*The Bible, Paten, and Chalice* [2] *shall mean while be brought by the Bishops who had borne them, and placed upon the Altar.*

*Then the Lords who carry in procession the Regalia* [3], *except those who carry the Swords, shall come from their places and present in order every one what he carries to the Archbishop, who shall deliver them to the Dean of Westminster, to be by him placed upon the Altar.*

## III. THE RECOGNITION

*The Archbishop, together with the Lord Chancellor, Lord Great Chamberlain, Lord High Constable, and Earl Marshal (Garter King of Arms preceding them), shall then go to the East side of the Theatre, and after shall go to the other three sides in this order, South, West, and*

[1] *The Theatre* is 'the Stage' of *Liber Regalis*. It is a platform set up at the crossing of the transepts, and has steps leading up to it on all sides. The Queen's Throne is placed on it, facing the Altar.

[2] *The Paten and Chalice* were known as 'St Edward's' up to 1649, when the ancient gold Paten and 'stone' Chalice were destroyed with the Regalia. The description 'St Edward's' first appears in the account of the Coronation of Eleanor of Provence, Queen of Henry III.

*The Bible* was not carried in procession until 1689.

[3] *The Regalia* were kept at Westminster Abbey up to the time of Charles II. The Convent of Westminster delivered them to the King in Westminster Palace on the morning of the Coronation, and the King or the Abbot of Westminster gave them to the Lords appointed to carry them in procession. The Regalia thus carried are:

| | |
|---|---|
| The Spurs, | The unpointed Sword, called *Curtana*, said to |
| The Sword of State, | signify Mercy, |
| The Armills, or Bracelets, | The pointed Sword, signifying Justice to the |
| The Sceptre with the Cross, | Temporalty, |
| The Rod with the Dove, | The pointed Sword, signifying Justice to the |
| The Orb, | Clergy, |
| St Edward's Crown, | St Edward's Staff. |

The Sovereign does not wear or carry the last four, although St Edward's Staff is in origin a walking-staff intended to be carried by the Sovereign, if he required support in the procession. The symbolical meanings have been attached to the Swords since the fifteenth century.

*North, and at every of the four sides the Archbishop shall with a loud voice speak to the People: and the Queen in the mean while, standing up by King Edward's Chair, shall turn and show herself unto the People at every of the four sides of the Theatre as the Archbishop is at every of them, the Archbishop saying:*

Sirs, I here present unto you Queen ELIZABETH, your undoubted Queen: Wherefore all you who are come this day to do your homage and service, Are you willing to do the same?

*The People signify their willingness and joy, by loud and repeated acclamations, all with one voice crying out* [1],

### GOD SAVE QUEEN ELIZABETH

*Then the trumpets shall sound.*

## IV. THE OATH

*The Queen having returned to her Chair, her Majesty having already on Tuesday, the 4th day of November, 1952, in the presence of the two Houses of Parliament, made and signed the Declaration* [2] *prescribed by Act of Parliament, the Archbishop standing before her shall administer the Coronation Oath, first asking the Queen,*

Madam, is your Majesty willing to take the Oath?

*And the Queen answering,*

I am willing.

*The Archbishop shall minister these questions; and the Queen, having a book in her hands, shall answer each question severally as follows:*

*Archbishop:* Will you solemnly promise and swear to govern the Peoples of the United Kingdom of Great Britain and Northern

---

[1] *The Recognition* is the completion of the Queen's election. The voice of the magnates has already been expressed at the Accession Council. At the Recognition the people give their consent by acclamation, the mediaeval form of which was, 'Yea, yea, yea, so be it, King N, King N'.

[2] *The Declaration* against Transubstantiation, Invocation of Saints, and the Sacrifice of the Mass, formerly made before the Oath at Coronation by Sovereigns from Anne to George III, after 1761 was made, more suitably, before both Houses of Parliament. By the Accession Declaration Act, 1910, the Sovereign is now required to declare only that he or she is 'a faithful Protestant'.

For *the Oath*, see above p. 24.

Ireland, Canada, Australia, New Zealand, the Union of South Africa, Pakistan and Ceylon, and of your Possessions and the other Territories to any of them belonging or pertaining, according to their respective laws and customs?

*Queen:* I solemnly promise so to do.

*Archbishop:* Will you to your power cause Law and Justice, in Mercy, to be executed in all your judgements?

*Queen:* I will.

*Archbishop:* Will you to the utmost of your power maintain the Laws of God and the true profession of the Gospel? Will you to the utmost of your power maintain in the United Kingdom the Protestant Reformed Religion established by law? Will you maintain and preserve inviolably the settlement of the Church of England, and the doctrine, worship, discipline, and government thereof, as by law established in England? And will you preserve unto the Bishops and Clergy of England, and to the Churches there committed to their charge, all such rights and privileges, as by law do or shall appertain to them or any of them?

*Queen:* All this I promise to do.

*Then the Queen arising out of her Chair, supported as before, the Sword of State being carried before her, shall go to the Altar, and make her solemn Oath in the sight of all the People to observe the premisses: laying her right hand upon the Holy Gospel in the great Bible (which was before carried in the procession and is now brought from the Altar by the Archbishop, and tendered to her as she kneels upon the steps), and saying these words:*

*The Bible to be brought*

The things which I have here before promised, I will perform and keep. So help me God.

*And a Silver Standish*

*Then the Queen shall kiss the Book and sign the Oath.*

*The Queen having thus taken her Oath shall return again to her Chair, and the Bible shall be delivered to the Dean of Westminster.*

38

# V. THE PRESENTING OF
# THE HOLY BIBLE[1]

*When the Queen is again seated, the Archbishop shall go to her Chair: and the Moderator of the General Assembly of the Church of Scotland, receiving the Holy Bible from the Dean of Westminster, shall bring it to the Queen and present it to her, the Archbishop saying these words:*

Our gracious Queen: to keep your Majesty ever mindful of the Law and the Gospel of God as the Rule for the whole life and government of Christian Princes, we present you with this Book, the most valuable thing that this world affords.

*And the Moderator shall continue:*

Here is Wisdom; This is the royal Law; These are the lively Oracles of God.

*Then shall the Queen deliver back the Bible to the Moderator who shall bring it to the Dean of Westminster, to be reverently placed again upon the Altar. This done, the Archbishop shall return to the Altar.*

# VI. THE BEGINNING OF THE
# COMMUNION SERVICE
## THE INTROIT
Psalm lxxxiv. 9, 10

Behold, O God our defender [2]: and look upon the face of thine Anointed. For one day in thy courts is better than a thousand.

*Then, the people kneeling, the Archbishop shall begin the Communion Service saying:*

Almighty God, unto whom all hearts be open, all desires known, and from whom no secrets are hid: Cleanse the thoughts of our

---

[1] *The Presenting of the Holy Bible* was introduced at the Coronation of William and Mary in 1689. From 1689 to 1937 the Presentation was made after the Putting on of the Crown. This is its first appearance in its present position. The making of the Presentation by the Moderator of the General Assembly of the Church of Scotland is a new feature.

[2] The anthem for *The Introit* is taken from the Introit of the 'Special Mass for the King' in *Liber Regalis*.

hearts by the inspiration of thy Holy Spirit, that we may perfectly love thee, and worthily magnify thy holy Name; through Christ our Lord. Amen.

*Archbishop*  Lord have mercy upon us.

*Answer*  Christ have mercy upon us.

*Archbishop*  Lord have mercy upon us.

Let us pray

O God, who providest for thy people [1] by thy power, and rulest over them in love: Grant unto this thy servant ELIZABETH, our Queen, the Spirit of wisdom and government, that being devoted unto thee with her whole heart, she may so wisely govern, that in her time thy Church may be in safety, and Christian devotion may continue in peace; that so persevering in good works unto the end, she may by thy mercy come to thine everlasting kingdom; through Jesus Christ, thy Son, our Lord, who liveth and reigneth with thee in the unity of the Holy Ghost, one God for ever and ever. R⁷ Amen.

## THE EPISTLE[2]

*To be read by one of the Bishops.*

I St Peter ii. 13

Submit yourselves to every ordinance of man for the Lord's sake: whether it be to the king, as supreme; or unto governors, as unto them that are sent by him for the punishment of evil doers, and for the praise of them that do well. For so is the will of God, that with well doing ye may put to silence the ignorance of foolish men: as free, and not using your liberty for a cloke of maliciousness, but as the servants of God. Honour all men. Love the brotherhood. Fear God. Honour the king.

---

[1] The Latin original of *the Collect*, 'O God, who providest for thy people', etc., is one of the prayers for the King in the Coronation Service of 973. It was adopted as the Collect in 1902. The present version is a more faithful rendering than that hitherto used.

[2] *The Epistle* and *the Gospel* are those appointed for the 'Special Mass for the King' in *Liber Regalis*. Except in 1685, when there was no Communion, this Epistle and Gospel have been read at most Coronations since the fourteenth century.

# THE GRADUAL [1]

Psalm cxli. 2

Let my prayer come up into thy presence as the incense: and let the lifting up of my hands be as an evening sacrifice. Alleluia.

## THE GOSPEL

*To be read by another Bishop, the Queen with the People standing.*

St Matthew xxii. 15

Then went the Pharisees, and took counsel how they might entangle him in his talk. And they sent out unto him their disciples, with the Herodians, saying, Master, we know that thou art true, and teachest the way of God in truth, neither carest thou for any man: for thou regardest not the person of men. Tell us therefore, What thinkest thou? Is it lawful to give tribute unto Cæsar, or not? But Jesus perceived their wickedness, and said, Why tempt ye me, ye hypocrites? Shew me the tribute-money. And they brought unto him a penny. And he saith unto them, Whose is this image and superscription? They say unto him, Cæsar's. Then saith he unto them, Render therefore unto Cæsar the things which are Cæsar's: and unto God the things that are God's. When they had heard these words they marvelled, and left him, and went their way.

*And the Gospel ended, shall be sung the Creed following, the Queen with the people standing, as before.*

I believe in one God the Father Almighty, Maker of heaven and earth, And of all things visible and invisible: And in one Lord Jesus Christ, the only-begotten Son of God, Begotten of his Father before all worlds, God of God, Light of Light, Very God of very God, Begotten, not made, Being of one substance with the Father, By whom all things were made: Who for us men, and for our salvation came down from heaven, And was incarnate by the Holy Ghost of the Virgin Mary, And was made man, And was crucified also for us under Pontius Pilate. He suffered, and was buried, And the third day he rose again according to the Scriptures, And ascended into heaven, and sitteth on the right hand

---

[1] *The Gradual* is derived from the same source. It has been restored to use for the present Coronation.

of the Father. And he shall come again with glory to judge both the quick and the dead: Whose kingdom shall have no end.

And I believe in the Holy Ghost, The Lord and giver of life, Who proceedeth from the Father and the Son, Who with the Father and Son together is worshipped and glorified, Who spake by the Prophets. And I believe one Catholick and Apostolick Church. I acknowledge one Baptism for the remission of sins. And I look for the Resurrection of the dead, And the life of the world to come. Amen.

## VII. THE ANOINTING[1]

*The Creed being ended, the Queen kneeling at her faldstool, and the people kneeling in their places, the Archbishop shall begin the hymn, VENI CREATOR SPIRITUS, and the choir shall sing it out.*

Come, Holy Ghost, our souls inspire,
And lighten with celestial fire.
Thou the anointing Spirit art,
Who dost thy seven-fold gifts impart.

Thy blessed Unction from above
Is comfort, life, and fire of love.
Enable with perpetual light
The dulness of our blinded sight.

Anoint and cheer our soiled face
With the abundance of thy grace:
Keep far our foes, give peace at home;
Where thou art guide, no ill can come.

Teach us to know the Father, Son,
And thee, of both, to be but One;
That, through the ages all along,
This may be our endless song:

Praise to thy eternal merit,
Father, Son, and Holy Spirit. Amen.

---

[1] The actual rite of the Coronation begins with *The Anointing*. The Recognition, the Oath and the Presenting of the Bible are in the nature of preliminaries.

*Veni, Creator Spiritus* was introduced into the Service in the fourteenth century, and makes its first appearance in *Liber Regalis*.

42

*The hymn being ended the Archbishop shall say:*

Let us pray

O Lord and heavenly Father, the exalter of the humble [1] and the strength of thy chosen, who by anointing with Oil didst of old make and consecrate kings, priests, and prophets, to teach and govern thy people Israel: Bless and sanctify thy chosen servant ELIZABETH, who by our office and ministry is now to be anointed with this Oil, and consecrated Queen: Strengthen her, O Lord, with the Holy Ghost the Comforter; Confirm and stablish her with thy free and princely Spirit, the Spirit of wisdom and government, the Spirit of counsel and ghostly strength, the Spirit of knowledge and true godliness, and fill her, O Lord, with the Spirit of thy holy fear, now and for ever; through Jesus Christ our Lord. R̷ Amen.

*Here the Archbishop is to lay his hand upon the Ampulla*

*This prayer being ended, and the people standing, the choir shall sing:*

I Kings i. 39, 40

Zadok the priest [2] and Nathan the prophet anointed Solomon king; and all the people rejoiced and said: God save the king, Long live the king, May the king live for ever. Amen. Hallelujah.

*In the mean time, the Queen rising from her devotions, having been disrobed of her crimson robe by the Lord Great Chamberlain, assisted by the Mistress of the Robes, and being uncovered, shall go before the Altar, supported and attended as before.*

*The Queen shall sit down in King Edward's Chair [3] (placed in the midst of the Area [4] over against the Altar, with a faldstool before it), wherein she is to be anointed. Four Knights of the Garter shall hold over*

---

[1] The prayer, 'O Lord and heavenly Father, exalter of the humble', etc., is a mutilated and altered form of the principal or consecratory prayer of *Liber Regalis*, in which its structure is modelled upon that of a Eucharistic Preface. In the Service of 973, the equivalent prayer is entitled 'The Consecration of the King'.

[2] The anthem, 'Zadok the priest', etc., was sung at the anointing of King Edgar in 973.

[3] *King Edward's Chair* is that popularly known as the 'Coronation Chair'. It was made by order of Edward I, to hold the 'Stone of Destiny' captured from the Scots in 1296. Before that year, the Stone was kept in Scone Abbey Church, and the Kings of Scotland were crowned in the chair in which it was enclosed.

[4] *The Area* is the term used to denote the Sanctuary of the church.

*her a rich pall of silk, or cloth of gold: the Dean of Westminster, taking*
*the Ampulla and Spoon from off the Altar, shall hold them ready,*
*pouring some of the holy Oil into the Spoon, and with it the Archbishop*
*shall anoint the Queen in the form of a cross:*

*On the palms of both the hands, saying,*

Be thy Hands anointed with holy Oil.

*On the breast, saying,*

Be thy Breast anointed with holy Oil.

*On the crown of the head, saying,*

Be thy Head anointed with holy Oil: as kings, priests, and
prophets were anointed:

And as Solomon was anointed king by Zadok the priest and
Nathan the prophet, so be thou anointed, blessed, and consecrated
Queen over the Peoples, whom the Lord thy God hath given thee
to rule and govern, In the Name of the Father, and of the Son,
and of the Holy Ghost. Amen.

*Then shall the Dean of Westminster lay the Ampulla and Spoon*
*upon the Altar; and the Queen kneeling down at the faldstool, the*
*Archbishop shall say this Blessing over her:*

Our Lord Jesus Christ, the Son of God [1], who by his Father was
anointed with the Oil of gladness above his fellows, by his holy
Anointing pour down upon your Head and Heart the blessing
of the Holy Ghost, and prosper the works of your Hands: that
by the assistance of his heavenly grace you may govern and preserve the people committed to your charge in wealth, peace and
godliness; and after a long and glorious course of ruling a temporal
kingdom wisely, justly and religiously, you may at last be made
partaker of an eternal kingdom, through the same Jesus Christ
our Lord.   R℣ Amen.

*This prayer being ended, the Queen shall arise and sit down again*
*in King Edward's Chair, while the Knights of the Garter bear away*
*the pall; whereupon the Queen again arising, the Dean of Westminster,*

---

[1] The prayer, 'Our Lord Jesus Christ, the Son of God', is the altered version
of a Latin prayer said after the anointing in the Service of 973 and in all subsequent
Services, English as well as Latin, up to 1661. The present version was made
by Compton for the Service of 1689.

44

*assisted by the Mistress of the Robes, shall put upon her Majesty the Colobium Sindonis [1] and the Supertunica or Close Pall of cloth of gold, together with a Girdle of the same. Then shall the Queen again sit down; and after her the people also.*

## VIII. THE PRESENTING OF THE SPURS AND SWORD[2], AND THE OBLATION OF THE SAID SWORD

*The Spurs shall be brought from the Altar by the Dean of Westminster, and delivered to the Lord Great Chamberlain; who, kneeling down, shall present them to the Queen, who forthwith sends them back to the Altar.*

*Then the Lord who carries the Sword of State, delivering to the Lord Chamberlain the said Sword (which is thereupon deposited in Saint Edward's Chapel) shall receive from the Lord Chamberlain, in lieu thereof, another Sword in a scabbard which he shall deliver to the Archbishop: and the Archbishop shall lay it on the Altar and say:*

Hear our prayers, O Lord [3], we beseech thee, and so direct and support thy servant Queen ELIZABETH, that she may not bear the Sword in vain; but may use it as the minister of God for the terror and punishment of evildoers, and for the protection and encouragement of those that do well, through Jesus Christ our Lord. R̵ Amen.

*Then shall the Archbishop take the Sword from off the Altar, and (the Archbishop of York and the Bishops of London and Winchester*

---

[1] For the *Colobium Sindonis*, the *Supertunica* and *Girdle*, see 'The Coronation Vesture', p. 31 above. The Dean of Westminster performs the function assigned in *Liber Regalis* to the Abbot.

[2] *The Presenting of the Spurs and Sword* is the first in the series of investitures with the Ensigns of Royalty which culminates in the Putting on of the Crown. The *Spurs* are first mentioned in connexion with the Coronation of Richard I in 1189. They were subsequently interpreted as emblems of knighthood. The *Sword* has been an Emblem of Royalty from Anglo-Saxon times. A sword was given to King Edgar at the Coronation of 973.

[3] The prayer, 'Hear our prayers, O Lord', etc., is an adaptation of the Blessing of the Sword in *Liber Regalis*. The form here used is taken from the Coronation Service of Queen Victoria. Queen Elizabeth I was girt with the Sword. Since the Coronation of Mary II with William III in 1689 no Queen has been girt with it, and the reference to girding, made in the prayer when the Sovereign is a King, is omitted at the Coronation of a Queen.

*and other Bishops assisting and going along with him) shall deliver it into the Queen's hands; and, the Queen holding it, the Archbishop shall say:*

Receive this kingly Sword[1], brought now from the Altar of God, and delivered to you by the hands of us the Bishops and servants of God, though unworthy. With this Sword do justice, stop the growth of iniquity, protect the holy Church of God, help and defend widows and orphans, restore the things that are gone to decay, maintain the things that are restored, punish and reform what is amiss, and confirm what is in good order: that doing these things you may be glorious in all virtue; and so faithfully serve our Lord Jesus Christ in this life, that you may reign for ever with him in the life which is to come. R̷ Amen.

*Then the Queen, rising up and going to the Altar [2], shall offer it there in the scabbard, and then return and sit down in King Edward's Chair: and the Peer, who first received the Sword, shall offer the price of it, namely, one hundred shillings, and having thus redeemed it, shall receive it from the Dean of Westminster, from off the Altar, and draw it out of the scabbard, and carry it naked before her Majesty during the rest of the solemnity.*

*Then the Archbishop of York and the Bishops who have assisted during the offering shall return to their places.*

## IX. THE INVESTING WITH THE ARMILLS[3], THE STOLE ROYAL AND THE ROBE ROYAL: AND THE DELIVERY OF THE ORB

*Then the Dean of Westminster shall deliver the Armills to the Archbishop, who, putting them upon the Queen's wrists, shall say:*

Receive the Bracelets of sincerity and wisdom, both for tokens of the Lord's protection embracing you on every side; and also

---

[1] The address, 'Receive this kingly Sword', etc., is an abridged version of the equivalent address in *Liber Regalis*.

[2] In the Service of *Liber Regalis* the Sword is not offered at the Altar until the Sovereign has received the Ring. The *Little Device*, or book of ceremonies, for the Coronation of Henry VII, directs the King to take back the Sword after offering it 'in token that his strength and power should come first from God and Holy Church'. The Sword was then redeemed. The present rubric dates from 1689.

[3] For the *Armills*, the *Stole Royal* and the *Robe Royal*, see pp. 31 f. above.

for symbols and pledges of that bond which unites you with your Peoples: to the end that you may be strengthened in all your works and defended against your enemies both bodily and ghostly, through Jesus Christ our Lord. ℞ Amen.

*Then the Queen arising, the Robe Royal or Pall of cloth of gold with the Stole Royal shall be delivered by the Groom of the Robes to the Dean of Westminster, and by him, assisted by the Mistress of the Robes, put upon the Queen, standing; the Lord Great Chamberlain fastening the clasps. Then shall the Queen sit down, and the Archbishop shall say:*

Receive this Imperial Robe, and the Lord your God endue you with knowledge and wisdom, with majesty and with power from on high: the Lord clothe you with the robe of righteousness, and with the garments of salvation. ℞ Amen.

## THE DELIVERY OF THE ORB

*Then shall the Orb [1] with the Cross be brought from the Altar by the Dean of Westminster and delivered into the Queen's right hand by the Archbishop, saying:*

---

[1] The *Orb* is considered by some historians of the Coronation to be another form of the Sceptre with the Cross. This view is supported by the Bayeux Tapestry, which represents Harold at his Coronation holding a rod in one hand and an orb with a cross in the other. On the other hand, an object like an orb, sometimes surmounted by a cross and sometimes not, and otherwise resembling the globe held by Fortuna and the Emperors in the pre-Christian Imperial coinage, appears in the hands of the Christian and later Byzantine Emperors in their portraits on coins, as well as in representations of Carlovingian rulers.

A rite for the Coronation of the Holy Roman Emperor directs that 'the Golden Pome with the Cross' be given to him after his Inthronization with the words, 'Receive the Golden Pome which signifies rule over all Kingdoms, In the name of the Father', etc.

The Orb appears in mediaeval representations of Kings of England, but, with two exceptions, it was not among the ornaments delivered at the Coronation until 1685. It is an item in the Stewart inventories of the Regalia, though not in earlier inventories. That it was not merely an iconographic attribute in the mediaeval period, however, is shown by the fact that, according to the fourteenth-century Westminster Missal, an orb surmounted by a cross should be buried with the King at his death; and at the Coronation of Richard III a similar orb was delivered in place of the Sceptre with the Cross.

*The Delivery of the Orb* is now no longer confused with the Investing with the Robe. The addresses recited at the two investitures are composed from the long address which accompanied the joint investiture in 1689.

47

Receive this Orb set under the Cross, and remember that the whole world is subject to the Power and Empire of Christ our Redeemer.

*Then shall the Queen deliver the Orb to the Dean of Westminster, to be by him laid on the Altar.*

## X. THE INVESTITURE PER ANNULUM, ET PER SCEPTRUM ET BACULUM

*Then the Keeper of the Jewel House shall deliver to the Archbishop the Queen's Ring* [1], *wherein is set a sapphire and upon it a ruby cross: the Archbishop shall put it on the fourth finger of her Majesty's right hand, and say:*

Receive the Ring of kingly dignity, and the seal of Catholic Faith: and as you are this day consecrated to be our Head and Prince, so may you continue stedfastly as the Defender of Christ's Religion; that being rich in faith and blessed in all good works, you may reign with him who is the King of Kings, to whom be the glory for ever and ever. R︠ Amen.

*Then shall the Dean of Westminster bring the Sceptre* [2] *with the Cross and the Rod with the Dove to the Archbishop.*

*The Glove, having been presented to the Queen, the Archbishop shall deliver the Sceptre with the Cross into the Queen's right hand, saying:*

Receive the Royal Sceptre, the ensign of kingly power and justice.

*And then shall he deliver the Rod with the Dove into the Queen's left hand, and say:*

Receive the Rod of equity and mercy. Be so merciful that you be not too remiss; so execute justice that you forget not mercy. Punish the wicked, protect and cherish the just, and lead your people in the way wherein they should go.

---

[1] *The Ring* has been delivered to the Sovereign at Coronation since 973. The address at the delivery, 'Receive the Ring of kingly dignity', etc., is a version, more faithful than that hitherto recited, of the address in *Liber Regalis*.

[2] The *Sceptre* and the *Rod* have been Ensigns of Royalty since the Coronation of 973. The Rod, which is slightly longer than the Sceptre and is tipped with a white enamelled dove, is sometimes called 'the Sceptre with the Dove'.

The Sceptre, the Rod and 'St Edward's Crown' were made for the Coronation of Charles II in 1661.

# XI. THE PUTTING ON OF THE CROWN

*Then the people shall rise; and the Archbishop, standing before the* St Edward's
*Altar, shall take the Crown into his hands, and laying it again before* Crown
*him upon the Altar, he shall say:*

O God the Crown of the faithful [1]: Bless we beseech thee this
Crown, and so sanctify thy servant ELIZABETH upon whose head
this day thou dost place it for a sign of royal majesty, that she
may be filled by thine abundant grace with all princely virtues:
through the King Eternal Jesus Christ our Lord.   R℣ Amen.

*Then the Queen still sitting in King Edward's Chair, the Archbishop,
assisted with other Bishops, shall come from the Altar: the Dean of
Westminster shall bring the Crown, and the Archbishop taking it of him
shall reverently put it upon the Queen's head. At the sight whereof the
people, with loud and repeated shouts, shall cry,*

## GOD SAVE THE QUEEN

*The Princes and Princesses, the Peers and Peeresses shall put on their
coronets and caps, and the Kings of Arms their crowns; and the trumpets
shall sound, and by a signal given, the great guns at the Tower shall
be shot off.*

*The acclamation ceasing, the Archbishop shall go on, and say:*

God crown you [2] with a crown of glory and righteousness, that
having a right faith and manifold fruit of good works, you may
obtain the crown of an everlasting kingdom by the gift of him
whose kingdom endureth for ever.   R℣ Amen.

*Then shall the choir sing:*

Be strong [3] and of a good courage: keep the commandments
of the Lord thy God, and walk in his ways.

*And the people shall remain standing until after the Homage be ended.*

---

[1] The prayer, 'O God, the Crown of the faithful', restores the Blessing of the
Crown discontinued in 1685.

[2] The address, 'God crown you', etc., is translated from a form which has been
in use since 973. Compton mutilated it out of all recognition, and successive
revisions removed from it such ancient elements as he had left. The original form
was restored in 1911. The acclamations after the crowning are an innovation
introduced by Compton in 1689.

[3] The anthem, 'Be strong', etc., is part of an anthem sung at this point of the
Service in *Liber Regalis*. In the Service of 973 it was sung at the girding on of
the Sword.

# XII. THE BENEDICTION

*And now the Queen having been thus anointed and crowned, and having received all the ensigns of royalty, the Archbishop shall solemnly bless her: and the Archbishop of York and all the Bishops, with the rest of the Peers, shall follow every part of the Benediction* [1] *with a loud and hearty Amen.*

The Lord bless you and keep you. The Lord protect you in all your ways and prosper all your handywork. R⁷ Amen.

The Lord give you faithful Parliaments and quiet Realms; sure defence against all enemies; fruitful lands and a prosperous industry; wise counsellors and upright magistrates; leaders of integrity in learning and labour; a devout, learned and useful clergy; honest, peaceable, and dutiful citizens.

May Wisdom and Knowledge be the Stability of your Times, and the Fear of the Lord your Treasure. R⁷ Amen.

The Lord who hath made you Queen over these Peoples give you increase of grace, honour, and happiness in this world, and make you partaker of his eternal felicity in the world to come. R⁷ Amen.

*Then shall the Archbishop turn to the people, and say:*

And the same Lord God Almighty grant, that the Clergy and Nobles assembled here for this great and solemn service, and together with them all the Peoples of this Commonwealth, fearing God, and honouring the Queen, may by the gracious assistance of God's infinite goodness, and by the vigilant care of his anointed servant, our gracious Sovereign, continually enjoy peace, plenty, and prosperity; through Jesus Christ our Lord, to whom, with the eternal Father, and God the Holy Ghost, be glory in the Church, world without end. R⁷ Amen.

---

[1] A *Benediction* of the Sovereign has followed the Investitures since the first English Coronation Service of 973. The present Benediction descends from the Service of 1685. It has been re-cast for the Service of 1953. The second clause, 'The Lord give you faithful Parliaments', etc., is newly written. From the twelfth century to 1831, the Sovereign kissed the Bishops after the Benediction. Queen Victoria discontinued the usage.

# XIII. THE INTHRONING[1]

*Then shall the Queen go to her Throne, and be lifted up into it by the Archbishops and Bishops, and other Peers of the Kingdom; and being enthroned, or placed therein, all the Great Officers, those that bear the Swords and the Sceptres, and the Nobles who carried the other Regalia, shall stand round about the steps of the Throne; and the Archbishop standing before the Queen, shall say:*

Stand firm, and hold fast from henceforth the seat and state of royal and imperial dignity, which is this day delivered unto you, in the Name and by the Authority of Almighty God, and by the hands of us the Bishops and servants of God, though unworthy. And the Lord God Almighty, whose ministers we are, and the stewards of his mysteries, establish your Throne in righteousness, that it may stand fast for evermore.   R̷ Amen.

# XIV. THE HOMAGE

*The Exhortation being ended, all the Princes and Peers then present shall do their Fealty and Homage publicly and solemnly unto the Queen: and the Queen shall deliver her Sceptre with the Cross and the Rod with the Dove, to some one near to the Blood Royal, or to the Lords that carried them in the procession, or to any other that she pleaseth to assign, to hold them by her, till the Homage be ended.*

*And the Bishops that support the Queen in the procession may also ease her, by supporting the Crown, as there shall be occasion.*

*The Archbishop first shall ascend the steps of the Throne and kneel down before her Majesty, and the rest of the Bishops shall kneel in their places: and they shall do their Fealty together, for the shortening of the ceremony: and the Archbishop, placing his hands between those of her Majesty, shall say:*

I GEOFFREY, Archbishop of Canterbury (*and so every one of the rest,* I N. Bishop of N., *repeating the rest audibly after the Archbishop*)

---

[1] At *The Inthroning* the Sovereign, having received all the Emblems of Royalty, is ceremonially placed in the Seat of Royalty. The address, 'Stand firm', etc., is an abridgement of the form recited from 973 to 1661, and modified in 1685. With the *Inthroning* the ceremonies of the Coronation are strictly ended. *The Homage*, which follows, is an addition of the fourteenth century. It is not an essential of the rite, and could be performed outside it.

will be faithful and true, and faith and truth will bear unto you, our Sovereign Lady, Queen of this Realm and Defender of the Faith, and unto your heirs and successors according to law. So help me God.

*Then shall the Archbishop kiss the Queen's right hand. After which the Duke of Edinburgh shall ascend the steps of the Throne, and having taken off his coronet, shall kneel down before her Majesty, and placing his hands between the Queen's, shall pronounce the words of Homage, saying:*

I PHILIP, Duke of Edinburgh do become your liege man of life and limb, and of earthly worship; and faith and truth I will bear unto you, to live and die, against all manner of folks. So help me God.

*And arising, he shall touch the Crown upon her Majesty's head and kiss her Majesty's left cheek.*

*In like manner shall the Duke of Gloucester and the Duke of Kent severally do their Homage. After which the Senior Peer of each degree (of the Dukes first by themselves, and so of the Marquesses, Earls, Viscounts, and Barons in that order) shall ascend the steps of the Throne and, having first removed his coronet, shall kneel before her Majesty and place his hands between the Queen's: and all the Peers of his degree, having put off their coronets, shall kneel in their places and shall say with him:*

I N. Duke, *or* Earl, *etc.*, of N. do become your liege man of life and limb, and of earthly worship; and faith and truth I will bear unto you, to live and die, against all manner of folks. So help me God.

*This done, the Senior Peer shall rise, and, all the Peers of his degree rising ·also, he shall touch the Crown upon her Majesty's head, as promising by that ceremony for himself and his Order to be ever ready to support it with all their power; and then shall he kiss the Queen's right hand.*

*At the same time the choir shall sing these anthems, or some of them:*

Rejoice in the Lord alway, and again I say, rejoice. Let your moderation be known unto all men: the Lord is even at hand. Be careful for nothing: but in all prayer and supplication, let your petitions be manifest unto God, with giving of thanks. And the peace of God, which passeth all understanding, keep your hearts and minds through Christ Jesu. *JOHN REDFORD*

O clap your hands together, all ye people: O sing unto God with the voice of melody. For the Lord is high and to be feared: he is the great King of all the earth. He shall subdue the people under us: and the nations under our feet. He shall choose out an heritage for us: even the worship of Jacob, whom he loved.
*ORLANDO GIBBONS*

I will not leave you comfortless. Alleluia. I go away and come again to you. Alleluia. And your heart shall rejoice. Alleluia.
*WILLIAM BYRD*

O Lord our Governour: how excellent is thy Name in all the world. Behold, O God our defender: and look upon the face of thine Anointed. O hold thou up her goings in thy paths: that her footsteps slip not. Grant the Queen a long life: and make her glad with the joy of thy countenance. Save, Lord, and hear us, O King of heaven: when we call upon thee. Amen.
*HEALEY WILLAN*

Thou wilt keep him in perfect peace, whose mind is stayed on thee. The darkness is no darkness with thee, but the night is as clear as the day: the darkness and the light to thee are both alike. God is light, and in him is no darkness at all. O let my soul live, and it shall praise thee. For thine is the kingdom, the power, and the glory, for evermore. Thou wilt keep him in perfect peace, whose mind is stayed on thee. *SAMUEL SEBASTIAN WESLEY*

*When the Homage is ended, the drums shall beat, and the trumpets sound, and all the people shout, crying out:*

## GOD SAVE QUEEN ELIZABETH
## LONG LIVE QUEEN ELIZABETH
## MAY THE QUEEN LIVE FOR EVER

*Then shall the Archbishop leave the Queen in her Throne and go to the Altar.*

# XV. THE COMMUNION

*Then shall the organ play and the people shall with one voice sing this hymn:* [1]

All people that on earth do dwell,
    Sing to the Lord with cheerful voice;
Him serve with fear, his praise forth tell,
    Come ye before him, and rejoice.

The Lord, ye know, is God indeed,
    Without our aid he did us make;
We are his folk, he doth us feed,
    And for his sheep he doth us take.

O enter then his gates with praise,
    Approach with joy his courts unto;
Praise, laud, and bless his name always,
    For it is seemly so to do.

For why? the Lord our God is good:
    His mercy is for ever sure;
His truth at all times firmly stood,
    And shall from age to age endure.

To Father, Son, and Holy Ghost,
    The God whom heaven and earth adore,
From men and from the Angel-host
    Be praise and glory evermore. Amen.

*In the mean while the Queen shall descend from her Throne, supported and attended as before, and go to the steps of the Altar, where, delivering her Crown and her Sceptre and Rod to the Lord Great Chamberlain, or other appointed Officers to hold, she shall kneel down.*

*The hymn ended and the people kneeling, first the Queen shall offer Bread and Wine* [2] *for the Communion, which being brought out of*

---

[1] The hymn, 'All people', etc., is an innovation of 1953. It replaces the Offertory anthem. It is a metrical version of Psalm c written by William Kethe, and published in 1562 by John Day in *The Whole Book of Psalmes*.

[2] The Queen's offering of the bread and the wine for the Sacrament at this point of the Communion Service is the survival of an ancient usage. In early times in the West, the communicants brought the elements for the Eucharist, and presented them to be offered as oblations on the altar. When the Mass was

*Saint Edward's Chapel, and delivered into her hands (the Bread upon the Paten by the Bishop that read the Epistle, and the Wine in the Chalice by the Bishop that read the Gospel), shall be received from the Queen by the Archbishop, and reverently placed upon the Altar, and decently covered with a fair linen cloth, the Archbishop first saying this prayer:*

Bless, O Lord, we beseech thee [1], these thy gifts, and sanctify them unto this holy use, that by them we may be made partakers of the Body and Blood of thine only-begotten Son Jesus Christ, and fed unto everlasting life of soul and body: And that thy servant Queen ELIZABETH may be enabled to the discharge of her weighty office, whereunto of thy great goodness thou hast called and appointed her. Grant this, O Lord, for Jesus Christ's sake, our only Mediator and Advocate. R⁷ Amen.

*Then the Queen kneeling, as before, shall make her Oblation, offering a Pall or Altar-cloth [2] delivered by the Groom of the Robes to the Lord Great Chamberlain, and by him, kneeling, to her Majesty, and an Ingot or Wedge of Gold of a pound weight, which the Treasurer of the Household shall deliver to the Lord Great Chamberlain, and he to her Majesty; and the Archbishop coming to her, shall receive and place them upon the Altar.*

*Then shall the Queen go to her faldstool, set before the Altar between the steps and King Edward's Chair, and the Duke of Edinburgh, coming to his faldstool set beside the Queen's, shall take off*

---

said at the instance of a particular person for that person's wellbeing, he or she offered the bread and wine. Early and mediaeval Service-books contain special Masses 'for Kings' of this description.

The Queen's oblation is presented in the chalice and paten carried in the procession.

[1] The prayer, 'Bless, O Lord, we beseech thee', etc., is a free rendering of one of the two 'Secret' Collects provided in *Liber Regalis*.

[2] The Queen's offering of an altar-cloth and a pound of gold is also a survival from the past. Sovereigns, noblemen, rich persons, etc., used to add to the oblations of bread and wine offerings of money or materials for the purposes of the Church, for the poor, or for some special cause. The collection of money for 'alms and oblations', prescribed in the Prayer Book Communion Service, is derived from this usage.

The rubric directing the Queen to kneel down 'at her faldstool set before the Altar' enjoins a departure from previous practice. Hitherto, after the Oblation, the Sovereign has returned to the Chair of Estate at the south side of the Altar.

*his coronet. Then shall they kneel down together; and the Archbishop
shall say this prayer* [1]:

Almighty God, the fountain of all goodness: give ear, we
beseech thee, to our prayers, and multiply thy blessings upon this
thy servant PHILIP who with all humble devotion offers himself
for thy service in the dignity to which thou hast called him.
Defend him from all dangers, ghostly and bodily; make him
a great example of virtue and godliness, and a blessing to the
Queen and to her Peoples; through Jesus Christ our Lord, who
liveth and reigneth with thee, O Father, in the unity of the Holy
Spirit, one God, world without end.   R⁷ Amen.

*Then shall the Archbishop bless the Duke, saying:*

Almighty God, to whom belongeth all power and dignity,
prosper you in your honour and grant you therein long to continue, fearing him always, and always doing such things as shall
please him, through Jesus Christ our Lord.   R⁷ Amen.

*Then the Archbishop, returning to the Altar, shall say:*

Let us pray for the whole state of Christ's Church militant here
in earth.

Almighty and everliving God, who by thy holy Apostle has
taught us to make prayers and supplications, and to give thanks,
for all men: We humbly beseech thee most mercifully to accept
these oblations, and to receive these our prayers, which we offer
unto thy Divine Majesty; beseeching thee to inspire continually
the universal Church with the spirit of truth, unity, and concord:
And grant, that all they that do confess thy holy Name may
agree in the truth of thy holy Word, and live in unity, and godly
love. We beseech thee also to save and defend all Christian Kings,
Princes and Governors; and specially thy servant ELIZABETH our
Queen; that under her we may be godly and quietly governed:
And grant unto her whole Council, and to all that are put in
authority under her, that they may truly and indifferently minister
justice, to the punishment of wickedness and vice, and to the
maintenance of thy true religion, and virtue.   Give grace, O

---

[1] The prayer for, and blessing of, a Queen's Consort at her Coronation is a
new feature. The prayer and blessing are new compositions.

heavenly Father, to all Bishops and Curates, that they may both by their life and doctrine set forth thy true and lively Word, and rightly and duly administer thy holy Sacraments: And to all thy people give thy heavenly grace; and specially to this congregation here present; that, with meek heart and due reverence, they may hear, and receive thy holy Word; truly serving thee in holiness and righteousness all the days of their life. And we most humbly beseech thee of thy goodness, O Lord, to comfort and succour all them, who in this transitory life are in trouble, sorrow, need, sickness, or any other adversity. And we also bless thy holy Name for all thy servants departed this life in thy faith and fear; beseeching thee to give us grace so to follow their good examples, that with them we may be partakers of thy heavenly kingdom: Grant this, O Father, for Jesus Christ's sake, our only Mediator and Advocate. R̷ Amen.

## THE INVITATION

Ye that do truly and earnestly repent you of your sins, and are in love and charity with your neighbours, and intend to lead a new life, following the commandments of God, and walking from henceforth in his holy ways: Draw near with faith, and take this holy Sacrament to your comfort; and make your humble confession to Almighty God, meekly kneeling upon your knees.

## THE GENERAL CONFESSION

Almighty God, Father of our Lord Jesus Christ, Maker of all things, Judge of all men: We acknowledge and bewail our manifold sins and wickedness, Which we from time to time most grievously have committed, By thought, word, and deed, Against thy Divine Majesty, Provoking most justly thy wrath and indignation against us. We do earnestly repent, And are heartily sorry for these our misdoings; The remembrance of them is grievous unto us; The burden of them is intolerable. Have mercy upon us, Have mercy upon us, most merciful Father; For thy Son our Lord Jesus Christ's sake, Forgive us all that is past; And grant that we may ever hereafter serve and please thee in newness of life, To the honour and glory of thy Name; Through Jesus Christ our Lord. Amen.

Almighty God, our heavenly Father, who of his great mercy hath promised forgiveness of sins to all them that with hearty repentance and true faith turn unto him; Have mercy upon you; pardon and deliver you from all your sins; confirm and strengthen you in all goodness; and bring you to everlasting life; through Jesus Christ our Lord. R7 Amen.

*Then shall the Archbishop say,*

Hear what comfortable words our Saviour Christ saith unto all that truly turn to him.

St Matthew xi. 28

Come unto me all that travail and are heavy laden, and I will refresh you.
St John iii. 16

So God loved the world, that he gave his only-begotten Son, to the end that all that believe in him should not perish, but have everlasting life.

Hear also what Saint Paul saith.

I Timothy i. 15

This is a true saying, and worthy of all men to be received, that Christ Jesus came into the world to save sinners.

Hear also what Saint John saith.

I St John ii. 1

If any man sin, we have an Advocate with the Father, Jesus Christ the righteous; and he is the propitiation for our sins.

*After which the Archbishop shall proceed, saying,*

Lift up your hearts.

*Answer:* We lift them up unto the Lord.

*Archbishop:* Let us give thanks unto our Lord God.

*Answer:* It is meet and right so to do.

*Then shall the Archbishop turn to the Lord's Table, and say:*

It is very meet, right, and our bounden duty, that we should at all times, and in all places, give thanks unto thee, O Lord, Holy Father, Almighty everlasting God:

Who hast at this time consecrated thy servant ELIZABETH to be our Queen, that by the anointing of thy grace she may be the Defender of thy Faith and the Protector of thy Church and People [1].

Therefore with Angels and Archangels, and with all the company of heaven, we laud and magnify thy glorious Name; evermore praising thee, and saying:

Holy, holy, holy, Lord God of hosts, heaven and earth are full of thy glory: Glory be to thee, O Lord most high. Amen.

## THE PRAYER OF HUMBLE ACCESS

We do not presume to come to this thy Table, O merciful Lord, trusting in our own righteousness, but in thy manifold and great mercies. We are not worthy so much as to gather up the crumbs under thy Table. But thou art the same Lord, whose property is always to have mercy: Grant us therefore, gracious Lord, so to eat the flesh of thy dear Son Jesus Christ, and to drink his blood, that our sinful bodies may be made clean by his body, and our souls washed through his most precious blood, and that we may evermore dwell in him, and he in us. R͞/ Amen.

## THE PRAYER OF CONSECRATION

Almighty God, our heavenly Father, who of thy tender mercy didst give thine only Son Jesus Christ to suffer death upon the Cross for our redemption; who made there (by his one oblation of himself once offered) a full, perfect, and sufficient sacrifice, oblation, and satisfaction for the sins of the whole world; and did institute, and in his holy Gospel command us to continue, a perpetual memory of that his precious death, until his coming again: Hear us, O merciful Father, we most humbly beseech thee; and grant that we receiving these thy creatures of bread and wine, according to thy Son our Saviour Jesus Christ's holy institution, in remembrance of his death and passion, may be partakers of his most blessed Body and Blood: who, in the same night that he was betrayed, (a) took Bread; and when he had given thanks, (b) he brake it, and gave it to his disciples, saying, Take, eat; (c) this is my Body which is given for you: Do this in remembrance of

(a) *Here the Archbishop is to take the Paten into his hands:*
(b) *And here to break the Bread:*
(c) *And here to lay his hand upon the Bread.*

---

[1] The Proper Preface, 'Who hast at this time consecrated', etc., is mainly a new composition.

(d) Here he is
to take the Cup
into his hand:
(e) And here
to lay his hand
upon the Cup

me. Likewise after supper (d) he took the Cup; and, when he had given thanks, he gave it to them, saying Drink ye all of this; for (e) this is my Blood of the New Testament, which is shed for you and for many for the remission of sins: Do this, as oft as ye shall drink it, in remembrance of me.  ℟  Amen.

*When the Archbishops and the Dean of Westminster, with the Bishops Assistant (namely, those who carried the Bible, Paten and Chalice in the Procession), have communicated in both kinds, the Queen with the Duke of Edinburgh shall advance to the steps of the Altar and both kneeling down, the Archbishop shall administer the Bread, and the Dean of Westminster the Cup, to them, and in the meantime the choir shall sing* [1] :  Psalm xxxiv, 8

O taste, and see, how gracious the Lord is: blessed is the man that trusteth in him.

*At the delivery of the Bread shall be said:*

The Body of our Lord Jesus Christ, which was given for thee, preserve thy body and soul unto everlasting life: Take and eat this in remembrance that Christ died for thee, and feed on him in thy heart by faith with thanksgiving.

*At the delivery of the Cup:*

The Blood of our Lord Jesus Christ, which was shed for thee, preserve thy body and soul unto everlasting life: Drink this in remembrance that Christ's Blood was shed for thee, and be thankful.

*After which the Queen and the Duke of Edinburgh shall return to their faldstools* [2] *; and the Archbishop shall go on to the Post-Com-munion, he and all the people saying:*

---

[1] The singing of an anthem at Communion time is an ancient usage. *Liber Regalis* directs that the Offertory anthem be sung again, with a slight change, at this point of the Service. The anthem, 'O taste, and see', etc., has no special connexion with Coronations. There has been no Communion anthem at the Coronation since 1661. Its revival is seemly, and has an obvious practical convenience.

[2] The rubric directing the Queen to return to her faldstool after reception of the Sacrament again enjoins a departure from usage hitherto followed. At previous Coronations, the Sovereigns have immediately resumed Crown, Sceptre and Rod, and have returned to the Throne. The Queen will now remain at her faldstool until the Post-Communion prayer has been said.

Our Father which art in heaven, Hallowed be Thy Name. Thy kingdom come. Thy will be done in earth as it is in heaven. Give us this day our daily bread. And forgive us our trespasses, As we forgive them that trespass against us. And lead us not into temptation, But deliver us from evil. For thine is the kingdom, The power and the glory, For ever and ever. Amen.

*After shall be said as followeth:*

O Lord and heavenly Father, we thy humble servants entirely desire thy fatherly goodness mercifully to accept this our sacrifice of praise and thanksgiving; most humbly beseeching thee to grant, that by the merits and death of thy Son Jesus Christ, and through faith in his blood, we and all thy whole Church may obtain remission of our sins, and all other benefits of his passion. And here we offer and present unto thee, O Lord, ourselves, our souls and bodies, to be a reasonable, holy, and lively sacrifice unto thee; humbly beseeching thee, that all we, who are partakers of this holy Communion, may be fulfilled with thy grace and heavenly benediction. And although we be unworthy, through our manifold sins, to offer unto thee any sacrifice, yet we beseech thee to accept this our bounden duty and service; not weighing our merits, but pardoning our offences through Jesus Christ our Lord; by whom, and with whom, in the unity of the Holy Ghost, all honour and glory be unto thee, O Father Almighty, world without end. Amen.

*Then, all the people standing, the Queen shall rise and, receiving again her Crown and taking the Sceptre and the Rod into her hands, shall repair to her Throne; and the Duke, putting on his coronet, shall return to his place.*

*Then shall be sung:*

Glory be to God on high, and in earth peace, good will towards men. We praise thee, we bless thee, we worship thee, we glorify thee, we give thanks to thee for thy great glory, O Lord God, heavenly King, God the Father Almighty.

O Lord, the only begotten Son Jesu Christ; O Lord God, Lamb of God, Son of the Father, that takest away the sins of the world, have mercy upon us. Thou that takest away the sins of the world, have mercy upon us. Thou that takest away the sins of the world, receive our prayer. Thou that sittest at the right hand of God the Father, have mercy upon us.

For thou only art holy; thou only art the Lord; thou only, O Christ, with the Holy Ghost, art most high in the glory of God the Father. Amen.

*Then, the people kneeling, the Archbishop shall say:*

Prevent us, O Lord, in all our doings, with thy most gracious favour and further us with thy continual help; that in all our works begun, continued, and ended in thee, we may glorify thy holy Name, and finally by thy mercy obtain everlasting life; through Jesus Christ our Lord. Amen.

The peace of God, which passeth all understanding, keep your hearts and minds in the knowledge and love of God, and of his Son Jesus Christ our Lord: And the blessing of God Almighty, the Father, the Son, and the Holy Ghost, be amongst you, and remain with you always.   R7 Amen.

*The solemnity of the Queen's Coronation being thus ended, the people shall stand, and the choir shall sing:*

## XVI. TE DEUM LAUDAMUS[1]

We praise thee, O God : we acknowledge thee to be the Lord.

All the earth doth worship thee : the Father everlasting.

To thee all Angels cry aloud : the heavens and all the powers therein.

To thee Cherubin and Seraphin : continually do cry.

Holy, Holy, Holy : Lord God of Sabaoth:

Heaven and earth are full of the Majesty : of thy glory.

The glorious company of the Apostles : praise thee.

The goodly fellowship of the Prophets : praise thee.

The noble army of Martyrs : praise thee.

---

[1] In 973 *Te Deum* was sung after the entrance into the church. In the twelfth century it was removed to a new position following the Benediction. There it remained until 1902. It is printed at this point in the Coronation Service of King Edward VII. The King's recent illness, however, made it necessary to shorten the Service wherever possible; in consequence *Te Deum* was sung at the end, as the royal procession moved into St Edward's Chapel. This arrangement was repeated in 1911 and 1937.

The holy Church throughout all the world : doth acknowledge thee;

The Father : of an infinite Majesty;

Thine honourable true : and only Son;

Also the Holy Ghost : the Comforter.

Thou art the King of Glory : O Christ.

Thou art the everlasting Son : of the Father.

When thou tookest upon thee to deliver man : thou didst not abhor the Virgin's womb.

When thou hadst overcome the sharpness of death : thou didst open the kingdom of heaven to all believers.

Thou sittest at the right hand of God : in the glory of the Father.

We believe that thou shalt come : to be our Judge.

We therefore pray thee, help thy servants : whom thou hast redeemed with thy precious blood.

Make them to be numbered with thy Saints : in glory everlasting.

O Lord save thy people : and bless thine heritage.

Govern them : and lift them up for ever.

Day by day : we magnify thee;

And we worship thy Name : ever world without end.

Vouchsafe, O Lord : to keep us this day without sin.

O Lord, have mercy upon us : have mercy upon us.

O Lord, let thy mercy lighten upon us : as our trust is in thee.

O Lord, in thee have I trusted : let me never be confounded.

## XVII. THE RECESS

*In the mean time, the Queen, supported as before, the four Swords being carried before her, shall descend from her Throne, crowned and carrying the Sceptre and the Rod in her hands, and shall go into the Area eastward of the Theatre; and, the Archbishop going before her, she shall pass on through the door on the south side of the Altar into St Edward's Chapel [1]; and after her shall follow the Groom of the Robes, the Lord Great Chamberlain and the Lords that carried the Regalia in the*

---

[1] *St Edward's Chapel* is so called because it contains the Confessor's tomb. A disrobing closet, formed by curtains and termed a 'traverse', is set up for the Queen in the Chapel.

procession (*the Dean of Westminster delivering the Orb, the Spurs and St Edward's Staff to the Bearers of them as they pass the Altar*); *and lastly shall go in the Dean. And,* TE DEUM *ended, the people may be seated until the Queen comes again from the Chapel.*

The Queen, being come into the Chapel, shall deliver to the Archbishop being at the Altar there, the Sceptre and the Rod to be laid upon the Altar: and the Archbishop shall receive the Queen's Crown and lay it upon the Altar also. Then, assisted by the Mistress of the Robes, and attended by the Lord Great Chamberlain and the Groom of the Robes, the Queen shall be disrobed of the Robe Royal and arrayed in her Robe of purple velvet.

Meanwhile the Dean of Westminster shall lay upon the Altar the Orb, the Spurs and St Edward's Staff, having received them from the Bearers of them, who shall then (preceded by the Bearers of the four Swords) withdraw from the Chapel by the same door on the south side and take the places assigned to them in the procession.

The Queen being ready, and wearing her Imperial Crown, shall receive the Sceptre with the Cross into her right hand and into her left hand the Orb [1] from the Archbishop, who having delivered them, shall withdraw from the Chapel and take his place in the procession: and the Lord Great Chamberlain shall do likewise.

Then her Majesty, supported and attended as before, shall leave the Chapel by the same door on the south side and shall proceed in state through the choir and the nave to the west door of the Church, wearing her Crown and bearing in her right hand the Sceptre and in her left hand the Orb.

And as the Queen proceeds from the Chapel, there shall be sung by all assembled:

## THE NATIONAL ANTHEM [2]

---

[1] If the Orb is a variant of the Sceptre with the Cross, the Queen is here made to carry two forms of the same thing. Richard III, who received the Orb at his Coronation, held it in his right hand, and carried the Sceptre with the Dove in his left. The Great Seal of Edward I represents that King as holding the Orb in his left hand and the Sceptre with the Dove in his right.

[2] The National Anthem has not before been sung at Coronations.

64

God save our gracious Queen,
Long live our noble Queen,
God save the Queen.
Send her victorious,
Happy and glorious,
Long to reign over us;
God save the Queen.

Thy choicest gifts in store
On her be pleased to pour,
Long may she reign.
May she defend our laws,
And ever give us cause
To sing with heart and voice
God save the Queen.

*finis*

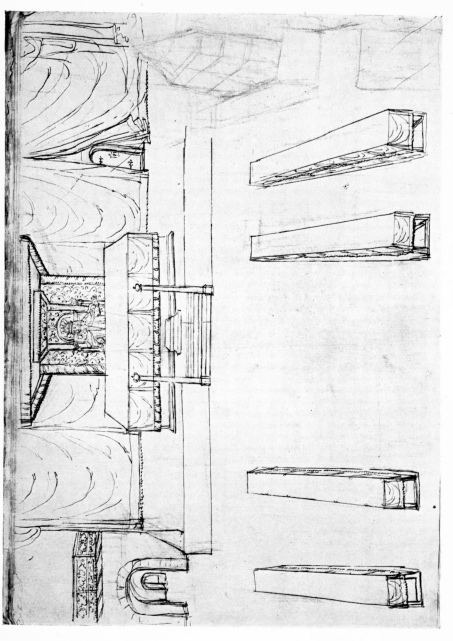

# APPENDIX

# THE CEREMONIAL DIRECTIONS OF 'LIBER REGALIS'[1]

## TRANSLATED INTO ENGLISH

This is the Order according to which the King must be crowned and anointed.

First, there is to be prepared a stage somewhat raised between the high altar and the choir of the church of Blessed Peter of Westminster near the four high pillars in the cross of the said church. At the ascent of the stage there are to be steps from the middle of the choir on the west side by which the Prince that is to be crowned can ascend to the said stage at his approach, when he passes through the midst of the choir. There are also to be steps on the eastern side by which the Prince can descend to the high altar, in front of the said altar, when he is about to receive with due devotion the solemnity of his holy anointing and coronation at the hands of the Metropolitan or Bishop that is to consecrate him.

PREPARATION OF THE CHURCH

In the midst of the said stage there shall be prepared a lofty throne, that the Prince may sit in it and be clearly seen by all the people.

The right of anointing the Kings and Queens of England belongs above all by ancient custom, hitherto followed, to the Archbishop of Canterbury, if he be present, and be of sound health. And if it happen that on account of bodily weakness or infirmity he cannot in his own person duly perform the ceremony, or if he be hindered by any other cause so that he cannot be present, another of the Bishops is to be found to perform the ceremony of unction and coronation, or one to whom the Metropolitan wishes to commit the said office.

Rights of the Abp of Canterbury

Now the King on the day before his coronation shall ride bareheaded from the Tower of London through the City to his Royal Palace of Westminster in suitable apparel, offering himself to be seen by the people who meet him.

PROCESSION ON THE DAY BEFORE CORONATION

---

[1] The Latin text and a full translation of *Liber Regalis* will be found in L. G. Wickham Legg's *English Coronation Records*, pp. 81–130. What follows is a slight revision of Mr Wickham Legg's version. The Roman numerals in brackets indicate the corresponding subdivisions of the Coronation Service of Queen Elizabeth II.

And it is to be noted that the coronation of the King and of the Queen must take place always on a Sunday or some Holy-Day.[1]

THE KING'S PREPARATION Now the said Prince on the night before the day of his coronation shall give himself up to heavenly contemplation and to prayer, meditating to what a high place he has been called, and how He through whom kings reign has appointed him in especial to govern his people and the Christian folk. And let him ponder on these words of the wise man: 'If thou be made the master, lift not thyself up, but be among them as one of the rest.'[2] And let him meditate that the royal dignity has been given to him by God as to a mortal man, and consider that he has been called to so high a position by God to be a defender of the Catholic Church, an extender of the Christian faith, and to protect, as far as he can, his realm and country which God has given into his charge. In his prayer he shall imitate the prudence of Solomon, who was bidden at the beginning of his reign to ask for whatever he desired; and he prayed, not for gold or silver, or riches, to be given to him or victory over his enemies, as a young man, but he rather asked that which God would give freely, and a man would receive with profit. 'Give me', said he, 'O Lord, an understanding heart, that I may be able to judge rightly and truly this people.'[3] And the Prince shall pray that the providence of God which has raised him to rule so great an empire be pleased to give him justice, piety, and wisdom; justice to his subjects, piety towards God, wisdom in the government of his kingdom, to the end that, softened by no favour, disturbed by no enemies, seduced by no lust, and hampered by no other passion, he may walk with firm foot in the paths of these virtues.

The duty of the Abbot of Westminster to instruct the King

And since it is necessary that the Prince should be informed about these and other observances which have to do with the coronation, the Abbot of Westminster of the time being shall be the Prince's instructor in these and other matters; and this office belongs to him alone.

And if the said Abbot be dead, and another have not yet been confirmed as Abbot of the same place so that he may rightly fulfil

---

[1] But the fifteenth-century Lincoln Pontifical used by Maskell in *Monumenta Ritualia Ecclesiæ Anglicanæ*, Vol. III, ed. 1882, contemplates the choice of an ordinary day.
[2] Ecclus. xxxii. 1.    [3] I Kings iii. 9.

this office, or if the Abbot be for any reason prevented from doing the office, then one shall be chosen, with the consent of the Prior and Convent of the said monastery, who shall be in all things fit to instruct the Prince, according to the manner and custom in use from the earliest times to the present.

On the day appointed on which the new King is to be consecrated, early in the morning the prelates and nobles of the realm shall assemble in the Royal Palace of Westminster to consider about the consecration and election of the new King, and also about confirming and surely establishing the laws and customs of the realm.

When this has been done with the agreement of all, a lofty seat shall be prepared in the royal hall,[1] and be suitably adorned with silken cloths of gold on which the King that is to reign is to be raised with all gentleness and reverence, after having first bathed as is the custom; and after being clothed with spotless apparel and shod only with socks. This is to be observed in every way, that as the Prince's body glistens by the actual washing and the beauty of the vestments, so his soul may shine by true and previous confession and penitence.

When these things have been duly performed, a procession shall be arranged in the church by the Archbishops, Bishops, and the Abbot and Convent of Westminster in silken copes with Gospel-books, censers, and the other things suitable to the procession, and so vested they shall go in procession to meet the King in the Palace. And the right of meeting the King that is to be with a solemn Procession belongs to the prelates of the realm and the monastery of Westminster alone, and they go before him to the church singing and chanting those anthems which are usually sung at the reception of Kings.

And Sir N. de Beauchamp of Bedford, who of old hath the office of Royal Almoner, shall cause a ray cloth or burell to be laid under the King's feet as he goes from his Palace to the stage in the church in Westminster, which has been prepared as is aforesaid. The stage and the steps on each side thereof must be spread all over with carpets prepared for this purpose by the King's servants. Around the top of the stage silken cloths of gold are to be hung.

[1] I.e. Westminster-Hall.

Now the throne in which the King must sit, and which has been mentioned before, must be covered wholly with silken and most precious coverings by the King's chamberlains; and cushions are also to be put by the chamberlains in the throne. But that part of the ray cloth or burell spread out by the aforesaid Almoner, as is described above, under the King's feet as he proceeds, which is inside the church, is given always to the use of the Sacrist; and the rest, which is outside the church, shall be distributed to the poor by the hands of the aforesaid Almoner.

THE KING'S
PROCESSION
TO WEST-
MINSTER
ABBEY
CHURCH

The King therefore that is to be crowned shall be preceded by the said prelates and monks; the Bishop of Durham and the Bishop of Bath in accordance with ancient custom, if they be present, shall support him on either hand.

The Chancellor, if he be a Bishop, shall go immediately before the King, vested in pontificals, with the stone chalice of St Edward from the Regalia. Before him shall go in like manner the Treasurer, if he be a Bishop or an Abbot, vested in pontificals, with the paten, which he shall hold likewise with great honour. This is the paten which is customarily held aloft by the sub-deacon before the altar at the Canon of the Mass.

But if it should happen that the Chancellor and Treasurer are not Bishops, other Bishops shall be appointed by the King, who, vested in pontificals in the manner described above, shall go before the King in the Procession with the chalice and paten.

In like manner, two other Bishops shall be appointed to support the King, if the Bishop of Durham and Bath be not then present.

After those who bear the chalice and paten, two dukes or more noble earls of the realm, and particularly those who by kinship are more nearly related to the King, shall follow immediately; one of them shall carry the royal Sceptre, on the top of which is placed a small cross. And the other shall bear the golden Rod with a dove on the top.

And the Abbot of Westminster, or the Prior, if the said Abbot be absent, shall deliver the chalice, paten, Sceptre and Rod to the said lords in the Palace; and they shall carry all these things in the Procession in the manner described.

Then shall follow three earls clothed in silk carrying swords. The Earl of Chester, who claims the first place in the carrying of the swords, shall bear the sword called *Curtana*. The Earl of Huntingdon shall carry another, and the Earl of Warwick shall carry the third.

Before these a noble appointed to the office by the King shall carry the great silk Spurs.

The square cloth of purple silk carried on four silvered lances with four bells of silver gilt shall be borne above the King wherever he goes by the Barons of the Cinque Ports, four of whom shall be assigned to each lance, by reason of the number of the Ports, so that no Port may appear to be preferred above another.

In like manner the same Barons shall carry a silken cloth over the Queen as she goes after the King, if she be crowned on that day. The said Barons shall keep these cloths by right of custom, but the lances and bells belong to the church of Westminster; so do the stage and all the carpets on it, with the silken cloths and cushions placed there by the King's servants, as is above described. These are to remain in the possession of the church where the King is crowned, in accordance with the ancient right and custom.

When all that appertains to the Procession has been duly arranged, as is described at length above, the Bishops and other prelates with the nobles of the realm and the said Convent of Westminster shall lead the King that is to be crowned from his Palace of Westminster to the church of St Peter of Westminster. And when he has been conducted through the choir and set on his seat on the stage, the Metropolitan, or Bishop that is to consecrate the King, shall address the people at the four sides of the stage, inquiring their will and consent about the consecration of the said King. The King meanwhile stands at his seat, and turns himself to the four sides of the stage, as the Bishop addresses the people, who give their consent, as is customary, and with loud and unanimous shouts exclaim, *So be it, So be it*, and *Long live the king*, uttering with great joy the name of the King. Then shall this anthem be sung by the choir:

ENTRANCE INTO THE CHURCH [II]

THE RECOGNITION [III]

*Let thy hand be strengthened*, etc.[1]

Then shall the Archbishop or Bishop that is to celebrate Mass vest himself before the high altar on account of the crowd that is come together, lest he should be hindered by it.

[1] Psalm lxxxix, part of 13 and 14.

When the Archbishop or Bishop is vested in pontificals, the Bishops of Durham and of Bath, or, in their absence, two other Bishops as has been said above, shall support the King on either side; and the other Bishops, with the Abbot of Westminster or other monk of the same monastery elected for this purpose, as is above described (who must be always at hand at the King's side to instruct the King in matters touching the solemnity of coronation, so that everything may be done aright), shall lead the King with honour from the said stage to the high altar.

THE FIRST OBLATION Then is the Prince bound to offer a pall and a pound of gold, fulfilling the commandment of Him who said: 'Thou shalt not appear empty in the sight of the Lord thy God.'[1]

And immediately thereupon the King shall lie prostrate upon the floor, which has been spread by the King's servants with carpets and cushions, and the Metropolitan or Bishop shall say this prayer over him:

*O God, who visitest the humble*, etc.

THE SERMON The prayer ended, the Metropolitan, or Bishop that is to consecrate the King, shall direct one of the Bishops to make a short and appropriate sermon to the people in a lofty place on the present matter, while the Metropolitan sits in his chair before the altar in the manner of a Bishop. Opposite to him the Prince that is to be crowned shall sit in a suitable chair prepared for him.

THE OATH [IV] The sermon ended, the Metropolitan or Bishop shall ask the King in a moderate and distinct voice:

*Sir, will you grant and keep*, etc.

(Here follows the Coronation Oath.)

There shall be added to the aforesaid questions what is right.[2] When all the above have been put, then the Prince, taking the Oath forthwith upon the altar in the sight of all, shall assert that he will keep all the above.

This done, the Metropolitan or Bishop shall kneel devoutly,

*Veni Creator Spiritus* [VII] and in a loud voice shall begin the hymn, *Come, Holy Ghost, our souls inspire*, while the King lies humbly on the carpets and cushions placed before the altar by his servants.

[1] Deut. xvi. 16.     [2] See p. 25 above.

After the hymn shall follow this prayer:

*We beseech thee, O Holy Lord, Father Almighty,* etc.

After the prayer, two Bishops or two cantors shall begin the Litany, while the Metropolitan or Bishop and the other Bishops with him shall prostrate themselves and recite by heart the seven penitential Psalms. THE LITANY [I]

[Here follow five prayers, the last of which, preceded by 'The Lord be with you', 'Lift up your hearts', etc., and introduced by the opening words of the Preface, 'It is very meet, right', etc., asks for the consecration of the King through the anointing which is to follow.] THE CONSE-CRATION OF THE KING

These prayers done, the Prince shall rise and sit in his chair before the Metropolitan or Bishop in the manner aforesaid. The Prince shall repose himself awhile in the chair, and then rise and go to the altar and lay aside his robes except his silken tunic and shirt, which are made to open wide at the breast, and between the shoulders, and on the shoulders, and also at the elbows. The openings of the tunic and shirt are tied together by silver loops.

Then the loops at the openings of the said tunic and shirt shall be undone by the Metropolitan or Bishop, while the canopy is stretched over the said Prince; and his hands shall be anointed with Oil, and the Metropolitan or Bishop shall say the prayer, THE ANOINTING [VII]

*Let these hands be anointed,* etc. on the Hands,

In the mean time the choir sings this anthem: *Zadok the priest and Nathan the prophet anointed Solomon King,* etc....

Then shall he be anointed on the breast, between the shoulders, on the shoulders, and both elbows with the same Oil, with which also a cross shall be made on his head; and afterwards he shall be anointed there with Chrism. on the Breast, etc., on the Head

And the Sacrist is to provide that the ampullas for the Oil and for the Chrism be ready, of which one is to be gilt and to contain the holy Chrism. But the other is to be of silver only, and to contain the Holy Oil.

When therefore the King has been thus anointed, the loops of the openings are to be fastened, on account of the anointing, by the Abbot of Westminster or by his deputy.

Then shall the following prayers be said by the Metropolitan:

*God, the Son of God, Jesus Christ our Lord*, etc.

INVESTITURE
*Colobium
sindonis,*
[end of VII] Then shall he be clothed in the *Colobium sindonis*, which is shaped like a dalmatic, after his head has been covered with a coif on account of the anointing.

The coif is to remain continuously on the King's head for seven days. And on the eighth day after the consecration of the King, one of the Bishops shall celebrate the Mass of the Trinity before the King in the church or in his chapel. And after Mass the Bishop shall take the coif from the King's head, and shall wash the King's head carefully with hot water, and after washing and drying it he shall reverently arrange the King's hair. Then shall he put the golden circlet on the King's head, with all honour; and the Prince shall wear the circlet bareheaded all that day in reverence of his cleansing.

[Blessing of
the royal
accoutre-
ments] These things having been executed in such manner, the royal accoutrements shall be blessed by the Metropolitan or Bishop:

*O God, the King of kings*, etc.

And after the accoutrements have been blessed, the King shall be clothed in his vesture by the Abbot of Westminster, or by his deputy, as has been mentioned before.

*Supertunica,*
[end of VII]
Buskins,
Spurs,
[VIII] And first he shall be clothed, over the *Colobium*, with a long Tunic reaching to the feet, wrought with golden figures before and behind; and buskins also and the Spurs shall be placed on his legs and feet.

Then shall follow the blessing of the Sword.

*Hear our prayers, we beseech Thee, O Lord*, etc.

Presenting of
the Sword,
[VIII] After, he shall receive the Sword from the Bishops: and let him know that with the Sword the whole kingdom has been entrusted to him to rule faithfully according to the following words. And the Metropolitan or Bishop shall say:

*Receive the Sword*, etc.

Armills,
[IX] When he has been girded with the Sword, he shall likewise receive the Armills; the Metropolitan or Bishop saying:

*Receive the Bracelets of sincerity*, etc.

These Armills shall hang like a stole round his neck, from both shoulders to the elbows, and shall be bound to the elbows by silken knots, as can be better seen from the manner in which the Armills are made.

Then shall he be vested in the Royal Pall, which is square and worked all over with golden eagles. Royal Robe [IX]

Then shall the Metropolitan or Bishop say:

*Receive this Pall, which is formed with four corners,* etc.

Then shall the Crown be blessed by the Metropolitan or Bishop, who shall say this prayer: Blessing of the Crown [XI]

*O God, the Crown of the faithful,* etc.

Then shall holy water be sprinkled on the Crown, and then the Metropolitan or Bishop shall cense the Crown, and set it on the King's head, saying:

*God crown thee with a crown of glory,* etc. Crown, [XI]

Afterwards, this anthem shall be sung:

*Be strong and of a good courage,* etc.

[The Blessing of the Ring follows.]
Then the Ring shall be given to the King by the Metropolitan or Bishop, who shall say:

*Receive the Ring of Kingly dignity,* etc. The Ring [X]

Then shall the King take the Sword wherewith he was girded and offer it to God upon the altar. The earl who is greatest of those present shall redeem it, and then carry it naked before the said King. The price of the Sword belongs to the altar. Oblation and Redemption of the Sword [VIII]

Then shall the Sceptre be put into his right hand. The Sceptre is of gold and has on the top a small cross. But before it is delivered the Gloves from the Regalia must be put on to the King's hands by the Metropolitan or Bishop, who shall say: Gloves,

*Receive the Sceptre, the ensign of kingly power,* etc.... Sceptre, [X]

After which the Rod, which is of gold and has a golden dove on the top, shall be delivered into his left hand by the Metropolitan or Bishop, who shall say: Rod [X]

*Receive the Rod of virtue and equity,* etc.

Then shall this Benediction be said over the King:

*The Lord bless you and keep you*, etc.

The Sacrist of Westminster is to take care that the royal accoutrements and the great Crown be early set with all honour upon the high altar, so that everything may be done without hindrance from the very great concourse of people which there is sure to be at such coronations.

[THE KISSING
OF THE
BISHOPS]

THE
INTHRONING
[XIII]
*Te Deum*
[XVI]

The King thus crowned, and vested with the Regalia by the Abbot of Westminster, and wearing the buskins, sandals, and Spurs, shall kiss the Bishops, who, with the other nobles of the realm, shall lead him to the Royal Throne, and the choir shall sing, *We praise Thee, O God*. When this hymn is ended, the Consecrator shall say:

*Stand firm, and hold fast from henceforth*, etc.

The King being thus set in his Throne, the peers of the realm shall stand around the king and stretch forth their hands as a sign of fidelity, and shall offer themselves to support the King and the Crown. And those especially who are near akin to the King shall lessen the King's labour in supporting the Crown, the Sceptre, and the Rod. But first of all the nobles of the realm then present shall publicly do their Homage on the stage.

(Directions are next given for the anointing and crowning of the Queen Consort. The ceremony having been accomplished, the *Liber* continues:)

Then when all these things have been done, the Office[1] of the Mass for the day's solemnity shall be begun by the cantors, if it happen that the coronation be performed on a Solemn Feast.

But if it chance that the coronation be performed on a simple Sunday, the Mass of the Sunday having first been celebrated by the Convent in due order, then shall the Mass for the King be begun....

The Offer-
tory, and
Second
Oblation of
the King,
and Oblation
of the Queen
[XV]

While the Offertory is in singing the King and Queen shall go from their Thrones, crowned, to the altar; and the King shall place in the hands of the Metropolitan or Bishop who is celebrating Mass the Oblation of bread and wine, after the example of Melchizedek.

Then shall he offer a mark of gold, and afterwards the Queen shall make her oblation....

[1] I.e. the Introit.

And when the King and Queen have received the Kiss of Peace, they shall come down from their thrones and go humbly to the altar to receive the Body and Blood of the Lord from the hands of the Archbishop or Bishop celebrating the Mass.

The Communion of the King and Queen

And when the King has received the Body, the Abbot of Westminster, or his deputy as aforesaid, shall minister to him the wine, to be used after receiving the Sacrament, from the stone chalice in the Regalia, and the said Abbot shall also minister to the Queen after the King as a sign of unity. For as in Christ they are one flesh by bond of marriage, so ought they to partake of the same cup. And the Body and Blood of Christ having been received by them, the King and Queen are to return immediately to their Thrones....

(At the conclusion of the Service the *Liber* directs as follows:)

RECESS [XVII]

The Mass ended, the King and Queen shall come down from their Thrones and go to the high altar. When they have come to the altar the Bishop who celebrated Mass, vested in the same pontificals that he wore before, with the ministers of the altar vested as before, and the torch-bearers and censer-bearers reverently going before him, shall go devoutly to the Shrine of St Edward, the King and Queen vested in their royal ornaments, with the Bishops and nobles following after him. And when they are come to the altar of the said shrine, the Bishop shall take off the Crowns from their heads, and set them on the said altar.

The putting off of the Crown, and the other royal ornaments

Then shall the Great Chamberlain of England strip the King of his regal ornaments, which shall be given severally to the Abbot of Westminster, or to his deputy, as has been often aforesaid, to be laid on the altar as they are taken from the King. And there shall be a closed place near the altar with curtains, prepared by the royal servants, where the King, stripped as aforesaid of his regal ornaments as far as his silken tunic and shirt, royal shoes and sandals, shall be clothed anew with other vesture by the said Great Chamberlain.

The King's Traverse in St Edward's Chapel

Meanwhile the Queen shall await the King at the said altar. And the King shall lay aside also the shoes and sandals which shall be restored entire to the Abbot of Westminster or to his deputy by the Great Chamberlain; and shall be shod with other shoes and sandals by the said Chamberlain.

The King therefore, clothed with honour in other vestments, as aforesaid, shall go humbly to the altar of the said shrine. And when he is come, the Archbishop or Bishop, vested in the same way as when he celebrated Mass, shall reverently set other crowns on the heads of the King and Queen. And they, thus crowned by the Archbishop, and carrying only the Sceptres from the Regalia in their hands, shall go up from the said Shrine by the high altar and stage, and shall return with great splendour through the midst of the choir by the same way as they came into the church, the aforementioned earls carrying the Swords. And it is to be noted that the outer garments which the King wears on that day before his coronation belong to the monk who is then Keeper of the Wardrobe of the monastery.

And provision is to be made by the King's servants on that day that the Convent of Westminster receive on the same day from the King a hundred bushels of corn and a modius of wine, and of fish as much as accords with the royal dignity. . . .

Immediately after the dinner, when the King has gone into his chamber, the Sceptres shall be delivered up to the Abbot of Westminster, or to another monk designated for this purpose by the King and Queen, that they may be with the rest of the Regalia in the said monastery, in accordance with the full recognition of the monastery, in Papal Bulls, in the Charters of Kings, and by ancient custom always observed, as being for ever the place of royal inauguration and coronation, and the repository of the regal insignia. It is upon this account that, in what is written in Papal Privileges and Royal Charters, the aforesaid church, that is, the church of Blessed Peter of Westminster, is named the Diadem of the Kingdom and likewise its Head and Crown, as though being that church which, alone among the other churches of England, is made illustrious by special prerogative.

On that day, the Earl of Leicester performs the service of Steward,[1] notwithstanding the claim of the Earl of Norfolk to that duty for himself.

[1] For the history and duties of this office and of those named below, see J. H. Round, *The King's Serjeants and Officers of State with their Coronation Services*, 1911.

*N* de Hastings shall perform the service of Naperer; he shall take for his own possession the napery removed after the dinner.

*N*. de Beauchamp of Dumelye,[1] to whom belongs the service of the Pantry, shall set on the salt-cellar and the knives.

The Earl of Arundel shall perform the service of Butler.

[1] A corruption of 'd'Elmley', the hereditary Worcestershire castle of the Beauchamp family; see Round, *op. cit.* p. 203.